HARDPRESS.NET
HOME OF HARD-TO-FIND BOOKS

The Lively Oracles Given to Us. or the
Christians Birth-Right and Duty, in the Custody
and Use of the Holy Scripture. by the Author of
the Whole Duty of Man
by Richard Allestree (D.D.)

Address:
HardPress
8345 NW 66TH ST #2561
MIAMI FL 33166-2626
USA
Email: info@hardpress.net

79.

Imprimatur.

JO. NICHOLAS.

Vice Cancell. *Oxon.*

Junii 10. 1678.

The lively Oracles given to us.
or.
The Christians birthright & duty, in the
custody & use of the holy Scripture

burg Sculp

THE
Lively Oracles given to us.
OR
The Christians Birth-right and Duty,
in the custody and use of the
HOLY SCRIPTURE.

By the Author of the WHOLE DUTY
OF MAN, &c.

Search the Scriptures, Jo. 5. 39.

At the THEATER in OXFORD, 1696.

THE

PREFACE.

IN the Treatise of the Government of the Tongue publish'd by me heretofore, I had occasion to take notice among the exorbitances of that unruly part, which sets on fire the whole course of nature, and it self is set on fire from hell, *Jam.* 3. 6. *of the impious vanity prevailing in this Age, whereby men play with sacred things, and exercise their wit upon those Scriptures*

The Preface.

Scriptures by which they shall be jug'd at the last day, *Joh.* 12. 48.

But that *Holy Book* not only suffering by the petulancy of the *Tongue*, but the malice of the heart, out of the abundance whereof the mouth speaks, *Mat.* 12. 34. *and also from that irreligion, prepossession, and supiness, which the pursuit of sensual pleasures certainly produces; the mischief is too much diffus'd and deeply rooted, to be controul'd by a few casual reflections. I have therefore thought it necessary, both in regard of the dignity and importance of the subject, as also the prevalence of the opposition, to attempt a profest and particular vindication of the Holy Scriptures, by displaying their native excellence and beauty, and enforcing the veneration and obedience that is to be paid unto them.*

This I design'd to do in my usual method,

The Preface.

*method, by an address to the af-
fections of the Reader; soliciting
the several passions of love, hope,
fear, shame and sorrow, which either the majesty of God in his sublime being, his goodness deriv'd to
us, or our ingratitude return'd to
him, could actuate in persons not utterly obdurate.*

*But whereas men, when they have
learnt to do amiss, quickly dispute and
dictate; I found my self concern'd to
pass sometimes within the verge of
controversy, and to discourse upon the
principles of reason, and deductions
from Testimony, which in the most
important transactions of human life
are justly taken for evidence. In which
whole performance I have studied to
avoid the entanglements of Sophistry,
and the ambition of unintelligible quotations; and kept my self within the
reach of the unlearned Christian Rea-*

der,

The Preface.

der, to whose uses, my labors have
been ever dedicated.

All that I require, is that men
would bring as much readiness to entertain the holy Scriptures, as they do
to the reading profane Authors ; I am
asham'd to say, as they do to the incen-
tives of vice and folly, nay, to the libels
and invectives that are levell'd a-
gainst the Scriptures.

If I obtain this, I will make no
doubt that I shall gain a farther point ;
that from the perusal of my imperfect conceptions, the Reader will
proceed to the study of the Scriptures themselves : there taft and see
how gracious the Lord is, *Pf.* 34. 8.
and, as the Angel commands Saint
John, *Rev.* 10. 9. eat the Book ;
where he will experimentally find
the words of David verified, Pf. 19. 7.
The Law of the Lord is an unde-
filed Law, converting the Soul : the
testimo-

The Preface.

teſtimony of the Lord is ſure, and giveth wiſdom to the ſimple. The Statutes of the Lord are right, and rejoice the heart; the commandment of the Lord is pure, and giveth light to the eies. The fear of the Lord is clean and endureth for ever, the judgments of the Lord are true and righteous altogether. More to be deſir'd are they than gold, yea, than much fine gold, ſweeter alſo than hony and the hony-comb. Moreover by them is thy ſervant taught, and in keeping of them there is great reward.

It is ſaid of Moſes, Ex. 34. 29. *that having receiv'd the Law from God, and converſt with him in Mount* Sinai *forty days together, his face ſhone, and had a brightneſs fixt upon it that dazled the beholders; a pledg and ſhort eſſay not only of his appearance at Mount* Tabor, Mat. 17. 1. *where*

at

The Preface.

at the Transfiguration he again was
seen in glory : but of that greater, *and
yet future change when he shall see
indeed his* God face to face, *and share
his glory unto all eternity.* The same
divine Goodness gives still his Law to
every one of us. *Let us receive it with
due regard and veneration ; converse
with him therein, instead of forty
daies, during our whole lives, and so
anticipate and certainly assure our interest in that great Transfiguration,
when all the faithful shall put off
their mortal flesh,* be translated from
glory to glory, *eternally behold their
God,* see him as he is, *and so enjoy
him.*

*Conversation has every where an
assimilating power, we are generally
such as are the men, and Books, and
business that we deal with :* but surely no familiarity has so great an influence on Life and Manners, as when
men

The Preface.

men hear God *speaking to them in his Word. That Word which the Apostle* Heb. 4. 12. *declares to* be quick and powerful, sharper than any two-edg'd sword, piercing to the dividing a-sunder of soul and spirit, and of the joints and marrow, and is a discerner of the thoughts and intent of the heart.

The time will come when all our Books however recommended for subtilty of discourse, exactness of method, variety of matter, or eloquence of Language ; when all our curious Arts, *like those mention'd* Act. 19. 19. shall be brought forth, and burnt before all men : *When the great Book of nature, and* heaven it self shall depart as a scroul roll'd together, *Rev.* 6. 14. *At which important season 'twill be more to purpose, to have studied well, that is, transcrib'd in practice this one Book, than to have run thro all be-*
                                    sides,

The Preface.

sides, for then the dead, small and great, shall stand before God, and the Books shall be open'd, and another Book shall be open'd which is the Book of Life, and the dead shall be judg'd out of those things which were written in the Books according to their works, *Rev.* 20. 21.

In vain shall men allege the want of due conviction, that they did not know how penal it would be, to disregard the Sanctions of Gods Law, which they would have had enforc'd by immediate miracle; the apparition of one sent from the other world who might testify of the place of torment. This expectation the Scripture charges every where with the guilt of temting God, and indeed it really involves this insolent proposal, that the Almighty should be oblig'd to break his own Laws, that men might be prevail'd with to keep his. But should he

The Preface.

he think fit to comply herein, the con-
defcention would be as fucceflefs in
the event, as 'tis unreafonable in the
offer. Our Savior affures, that they
who hear not *Mofes* and the Prophets, *the inftructions and commands
laid down in holy Scripture, would
not be wrought upon by any other method,* would not be perfwaded *by that
which they allow for irrefiftable conviction,* tho one rofe again from the
dead, *Luke.* 16. 31.

The

THE
LIVELY ORACLES
GIVEN TO US,

Or the Christians Birth-right and Duty in the cuſtody and uſe of the

HOLY SCRIPTURE.

SECT I.

The ſeveral Methods of Gods communicating the knowledg of himſelf.

GOD, as he is inviſible to human eyes, ſo is he unfathomable by human underſtandings; the perfection of his nature, and the impotency of ours, ſetting us at too great a diſtance to have any clear perception of him. Nay, ſo far are we from a full comprehenſion, that we can diſcern nothing at all of him, but by his own light; thoſe diſcoveries he hath bin pleas'd to make of himſelf.

2. THOSE have bin of ſeveral ſorts; The firſt was by infuſion in mans creation, when

A   God

God interwove into mans very conftitution and being the notions and apprehenfions of a Deity: and at the fame inftant when he breath'd into him a living foul, impreft on it that native religion, which taught him to know and reverence his Creator, which we may call the inftinct of humanity. Nor were thofe principles dark and confus'd, but clear and evident, proportionable to the ends they were defign'd to, which were not only to contemplate the nature, but to do the will of God; practice being even in the ftate of innocence preferable before an unactive fpeculation.

3. But this Light being foon eclips'd by *Adams* difobedience, there remain'd to his benighted pofterity, only fome faint glimmerings, which were utterly infufficient to guide them to their end, without frefh aids, and renew'd manifeftations of God to them. It pleas'd God therefore to repair this ruine, and by frequent revelations to communicate himfelf to the Patriarchs in the firft Ages of the World; afterwards to Prophets, and other holy men; till at laft he revealed himfelf yet more illuftrioufly *in the face of Jefus Chrift*, 2 Cor. 4. 6.

4. This is the one great comprehenfive Revelation wherein all the former were involv'd, and to which they pointed; the whole myftery of Godlinefs being compris'd in this

of

of *Gods* being *manifested in the flesh*, and the consequents thereof. 1 *Tim.* 3. 16. whereby our Savior as he effected our reconciliation with God by the sacrifice of his death; so he declar'd both that, and all things else that it concern'd man to know in order to bliss, in his doctrin and holy life. And this *Teacher* being not only *sent from God*, Jo. 3. but being himself God blessed for ever; it cannot be that his instructions can want any supplement. Yet that they might not want attestation neither to the incredulous world; he confirm'd them by the repeated miracles of his life, and by the testimony of those who saw the more irrefragable conviction of his Resurrection and Ascension. And that they also might not want credit and enforcement, the holy Spirit set to his seal, and by his miraculous descent upon the Apostles, both asserted their commission, and enabled them for the discharge of it, by all gifts necessary for the propagating the Faith of Christ over the whole World.

5. THESE were the waies by which God was pleased to reveal himself to the Forefathers of our Faith, and that not only for their sakes, but ours also, to whom they were to derive those divine dictates they had receiv'd. Saint *Stephen* tells us, those under the Law *receiv'd the lively Oracles* to deliver down to their posterity, *Acts* 7. 38. And those un-

A 2   der

der the Gospel, who receiv'd yet more lively
Oracles from him who was both the Word
and the Life, did it for the like purpose; to
transmit it to us upon whom the ends of the
world are come. By this all need of repeated
Revelations is superseded, the faithful deri-
ving of the former, being sufficient to us for
all things that appertain to life and godliness,
2 pet. 1. 3.

6. AND for this, God (whose care is equal
for all successions of men) hath graciously
provided, by causing Holy Scriptures to be
writ; by which he hath deriv'd on every succeeding Age the illuminations of the former. And for that purpose endowed the
Writers not only with that moral fidelity
requisite to the truth of History, but with a
divine Spirit, proportionable to the great design of fixing an immutable rule for Faith
and Manners. And to give us the fuller security herein, he has chosen no other pen-
men of the New Testament, than those who
were the first oral Promulgers of our Christian Religion; so that they have left to us
the very same doctrin they taught the Primitive Christians; and he that acknowledges
them divinely inspir'd in what they preach'd,
cannot doubt them to be so in what they
writ. So that we all may injoy virtually and
effectively that wish of the devout Father,
who desir'd to be St. *Paul*'s Auditor: for he
that

that hears any of his Epiftles read, is as really
fpoke to by Saint *Paul*, as thofe who were
within the found of his voice.   *Thus God, who
in times paft fpake at fundry times, and in diverfe
manners to our Fathers by the Prophets, and in
the latter days by his fon,* Heb. 1. 1, 2. conti-
nues ftill to fpeak to us by thefe infpir'd Writers; and what Chrift once faid to his Difciples in relation to their preaching is no lefs
true of their writings : *He that defpifeth you, defpifeth me,* Luk. 10. 16.   All the contemt that
is at any time flung on thefe facred Writings,
rebounds higher, and finally devolves on the
firft Author of thofe doctrins, whereof thefe
are the Regifters and Tranfcripts.

7. But this is a guilt which one would
think peculiar to Infidels and Pagans, and not
incident to any who had in their Baptifm
lifted themfelves under Chrifts banner : yet I
fear I may fay, of the two parties, the Scripture has met with the worft treatment from
the latter. For if we meafure by the frequency and variety of injuries, I fear Chriftians will
appear to have out-vied Heathens : Thefe
bluntly disbelieve them, neglect, nay perhaps
fcornfully deride them.   Alas, Chriftians do
this and more; they not only put contemts, but
tricks upon the Scripture, wreft and diftort it
to juftify all their wild phancies, or fecular defigns; and fuborn its Patronage to thofe things
it forbids, and tells us that God abhors.

8. In-

8. Indeed ſo many are the abuſes we offer it, that he that conſiders them would ſcarce think we own'd it for the words of a ſenſible man, much leſs of the great omniſcient God. And I believe 'twere hard to aſſign any one ſo comprehenſive and efficacious cauſe of the univerſal depravation of manners, as the diſvaluing of this divine Book, which was deſign'd to regulate them. It were therefore a work worthy another inſpired writing, to attemt the reſcue of this, and recover it to its juſt eſtimate. Yet alas, could we hope for that, we have ſcoffers who would as well deſpiſe the New as the Old; and like the Huſbandmen in the Goſpel, *Mat.* 21. 36. would anſwer ſuch a ſucceſſion of meſſages by repeating the ſame injuries.

9. To ſuch as theſe 'tis I confeſs vain for man to addreſs; nay 'twere inſolence to expect that human Oratory ſhould ſucceed where the divine fails; yet the ſpreading infection of theſe renders it neceſſary to adminiſter antidotes to others. And beſides, tho (God be bleſt) all are not of this form, yet there are many who, tho not arriv'd to this contemt, yet want ſome degrees of that juſt reverence they owe the ſacred Scriptures, who give a confus'd general aſſent to them as the word of God, but afford them not a conſideration and reſpect anſwerable to ſuch an acknowledgment. To ſuch as theſe, I ſhall hope

it

it may not be utterly vain to attemt the exciting of those drowsy notions that lie unactive in them; by presenting to them some considerations concerning the excellence and use of the Scripture: which being all but necessary consequences of that principle they are supposed to own, *viz.* that they are Gods word, I cannot much question their assent to the speculative part: I wish I could as probably assure my self of the practic.

10. INDEED were there nothing else to be said in behalf of holy Writ, but that it is Gods word, that were enough to command the most awful regard to it.   And therefore it is but just we make that the first and principal consideration in our present discourse.   But then 'tis impossible that that can want others to attend it; since whatsoever God saies, is in all respects compleatly good.   I shall therefore to that of its divine original add secondly the consideration of its subject Matter; thirdly, of its excellent and no less diffusive end and design; and fourthly, of its exact propriety and fitness to that design: which are all such qualifications, that where they concur, nothing more can be requir'd to commend a writing to the esteem of rational men.   And upon all these tests, notwithstanding the cavil of the Romanists and others, whose force we shall examin with the unhappy issue of contrary counsels, this law of God
will

will be found to anſwer the Pſalmiſts character of it *Pſ.* 19. 7. *The Law of God is perfect*:
and 'twill appear that the cuſtody and uſe
thereof is the Birth-right and Duty of every
Chriſtian.   All which ſeverals being faithfully deduced, it will only remain that I add
ſuch cautions as will be neceſſary to the due
performance of the aforeſaid duty, and our
being in ſome degree render'd perfect, as this
Law of God, and the Author thereof himſelf
is perfect, *Mat.* 5. 48.

SECT.

SECT. II.

The divine Original, Endearments, and Authority of the Holy Scripture.

MENS judgments are so apt to be biast by their affections, that we often find them readier to confider who fpeaks, than what is fpoken: a temper very unfafe, and the principle of great injuftice in our infe- rior tranfactions with men; yet here there are very few of us that can wholly diveft our felves of it, whereas, when we deal with God (in whom alone an implicit faith may fe- curely be repofed) we are nice and wary, bring our fcales and meafures, will take no- thing upon his word which holds not weight in our own balance. 'Tis true, he needs not our partiality to be *juftified in his fayings,* Pfal. 51. 4. *His words are pure, even as the filver tried feven times in the fire,* Pfal. 12. 6. able to pafs the ftricteft teft that right reafon (truly fo called) can put them to. Yet it fhews a great perverfenefs in our nature, that we who fo eafily refign our underftandings to fallible men, ftand thus upon our guard againft God; make him difpute for every inch he gains on us; nor will afford him what we daily grant

B

to

to any credible man, to receive an affirmation upon truft of his veracity.

2. I am far from contradicting our Saviors Precept, of *Search the Scriptures*, Jo. 7. or Saint *Pauls*, of *proving all things*, 1 Thef. 5. 21, we cannot be too induftrious in our inqueft after truth, provided we ftill referve to God the decifive vote, and humbly acquiefce in his fenfe, how diftant foever from our own; fo that when we confult Scripture (I may add reafon either) 'tis not to refolve us whether God be to be believed or no in what he has faid, but whether he hath faid fuch and fuch things : for if we are convinc'd he have ; reafon as well as Religion commands our affent.

3. WHATEVER therefore God has faid, we are to pay it a reverence merely upon the account of its Author, over and above what the excellence of the matter exacts: and to this we have all inducements as well as obligation : there being no motives to render the words of men eftimable to us, which are not eminently and tranfcendently applicable to thofe of God.

4. THOSE motives we may reduce to four : firft, the Autority of the Speaker ; fecondly, his Kindnefs ; thirdly, his Wifdom ; and fourthly, his Truth. Firft, for that of Autority : that may be either native, or acquired ; the native is that of a parent, which is fuch a charm
of

of obfervance, that we fee *Solomon*, when he would imprefs his counfels, affumes the perfon of a Father; *Hear O my children the inftructions of a Father*, Prov. 4. 1. And generally thro that whole Book he ufes the compellation of my Son, as the greateft endearment to engage attention and reverence. Nay fo indifpenfible was the obligation of children in this refpect, that we fee the contumacious child that would not hearken to the advice of his Parents, was by God himfelf adjudged to death, *Deut.* 21. 20.

5. NOR have only Gods, but mens Laws exacted that filial reverence to the dictates of Parents. But certainly no Parent can pretend fuch a title to it as God, who is not only the immediate Father of our perfons, but the original Father of our very nature; not only of our flefh, but of our fpirits alfo, *Heb.* 12. 9. So that the Apoftles Antithefis in that place is as properly applied to counfels as corrections; and we may as rightly infer, that if we give reverence to the advices of our earthly Parents, *much more ought we fubject our felves to this Father of our fpirits.* And we have the very fame reafon wherewith to enforce it: for *the Fathers of our flefh do* as often dictate, *as correct according to their own pleafures*, prefcribe to their children not according to the exact meafures of right and wrong, but after that humor which moft predom-

dominates in themſelves. But God alwaies directs his admonitions to our profit, *that we may be partakers of his holineſs*, Heb. 12. 10. So that we are as unkind to our ſelves, as irreverent towards him, whenever we let any of his words fall to the ground; whoſe claim to this part of our reverence is much more irrefragable than that of our natural Parents.

6. B u t beſides this native Autority there is alſo an acquired; and that we may diſtinguiſh into two ſorts: the one of dominion, the other of reputation. To the firſt kind belongs that of Princes, Magiſtrates, Maſters, or any that have coercive power over us. And our own intereſt teaches us not to ſlight the words of any of theſe, who can ſo much to our coſt ſecond them with deeds. Now God has all theſe titles of juriſdiction; He is the great King, *Pſal.* 48. 2. Nor was it only a complement of the Pſalmiſts; for himſelf owns the ſtile, *I am a great King*, Mal. 1. *He is the Judge of all the World*, Gen. 18. yea, that *Ancient of daies*, before whom the Books were open'd, *Dan.* 7. 13. He is our Lord and Maſter by right, both of Creation and Redemtion; and this Chriſt owns even in his ſtate of inanition; yea, when he was about the moſt ſervile emploiment, the waſhing his Diſciples feet, when he was moſt literally in the form of a ſervant; yet he ſcruples not to aſſert his right to that oppoſite title; *You call me Maſter,*
and

and Lord; and ye say well, for so I am; Jo. 13. 13. Nor are these emty names, but effectively attended with all the power they denote. Yet so stupid are we, that whilst we awfully receive the dictates of our earthly Superiors, we slight and neglect the Oracles of that God who is King of Kings, and Lord of Lords. When a Prince speaks, we are apt to cry out with *Herods* Flatterers, *the voice of a God, and not of a man,* Acts 12. Yet when it is indeed the voice of God, we choose to listen to any thing else rather than it. But let us sadly remember, that notwithstanding our contemts, this word shall (as our Savior tells us) *judg us at the last day,* Jo. 12. 48.

7. A second sort of acquir'd Autority is that of reputation. When a man is famed for some extraordinary excellencies, whether moral or intellectual, men come with appetite to his discourses, greedily suck them in, nor need such a one bespeak attention; his very name has done it for him, and prepossest him of his Auditors regard. Thus the Rabbies among the Jews, the Philosophers among the Greeks, were listened to as Oracles, and to cite them was (by their admiring Disciples) thought a concluding Argument. Nay, under Christianity, this admiration of mens persons has bin so inordinate, that it has crumbled Religion away in little insignificant parties; whilst non only *Paul, Apollo* or *Cephas,*

Cephas, but names infinitly inferior, have become the diftinctive characters of Sects and feparate Communions. So eafily alas are we charm'd by our prepoffeffions, and with itching ears run in queft of thofe doctrines which the fame of their Authors, rather than the evidence of truth, commends to us.

8. AND hath God done nothing to get him a repute among us? has he no excellencies to deferve our efteem? is he not worthy to prefcribe to his own creatures? If we think yes, why is he the only perfon to be difregarded? or why do we fo unfeafonably depart from our own humor, as not to give his Word a reverence proportionable to that we pretend for him; nay, which we actually pay to men of like paffions with our felves? A contemt fo abfurd as well as impious, that we have not the example of any the moft barbarous people to countenance us. For tho fome of them have made very wild miftakes in the choice of their Deities, yet they have all agreed in this common principle, that whatever thofe Deities faid, was to be receiv'd with all poffible veneration; yea, fuch a deference gave they to all fignifications of the divine will, that as they would undertake no great enterprize without confulting their Auguries; fo upon any inaufpicious figns they relinquifht their attemts. And certainly if we had the fame reverence for the true God
which

which they had for the false, we should as frequently consult him. We may do it with much more ease and certainty: we need not trust to the entrails of Beasts, or motion of Birds: we need not go to *Delphos*, or the Lybian *Hammon* for the resolving our doubts: but what *Moses* said to *Israel* is very applicable to us, *the Word is nigh thee*, Deut. 30. 14. That Word which *David* made his *Counsellor*, Psal. 119. 24. his *Comforter*, ver. 50. his *Treasure*, ver. 72. his *Study*, ver. 99. And had we those awful apprehensions of God which he had, we should pay the like reverence to his Word. Did we well ponder how many titles of Autority he has over us, we should surely by asham'd to deny that respect to him in whom they all conspire, which we dare not deny to them separately in human Superiors.

9. A second motive to esteem mens words, is the kindness of the speaker. This has such a fascinating power, as nothing but extreme ill nature can resist. When a man is assur'd of the kindness of him that speaks, whatever is spoken is taken in good part. This is it that distinguishes the admonitions of a friend from the reproaches of an enemy; and we daily in common conversation receive those things with contentment and applause from an intimate and familiar, which if spoken by a stranger or enemy would be despis'd

defpis'd or ftomach'd. So infinuating a thing is kindnefs, that where it has once got it felf believ'd, nothing it faies after is difputed; it fupples the mind, and makes it ductile and pliant to any impreffions.

10. But what human kindnefs is there that can come in any competition with the Divine? it furpaffes that of the neareft and deareft relations; *Mothers may forget, yet will I not forget thee,* Ifa. 49. 15. And the Pfalmift found it experimentally true, *When my Father and my Mother forfake me, the Lord taketh me up,* Pf. 27. 10. The tendereft bowels compared to his, are adamant and flint: fo that 'tis a moft proper epithet the Wife man gives him, *O Lord thou lover of fouls,* Wif. 11. 26. Nor is this affection merely mental: but it attefts it felf by innumerable effects. The effects of love are all reducible to two heads, doing and fuffering; and by both thefe God has moft eminently attefted his love to us.

11. For the firft, we cannot look either on our bodies or our fouls, on the whole Univerfe about us, or that better World above us; but we fhall in each fee *the Lord hath done great things for us,* Pfal, 126. Nay, not only our enjoyments, but even the capacity to enjoy, is his bounty. Had not he drawn mankind out of his original clay, what had we bin concern'd in all the other works of his Creation? So that if we put any value either upon what

we

we have or what we are, we cannot but account our selves so much indebted to this his active love. And tho the passive was not practicable by the divine Nature simply and apart, yet that we might not want all imaginable evidences of his love, he who was God blessed for ever, linkt his impassible to our passible nature; assum'd our humanity, that he might espouse our sorrows, and was born on purpose that he might die for us. So that sure we may say in his own words, *greater love than this hath no man*; Jo. 15. 13.

12. AND now tis very hard, if such an unparallel'd love in God, may not as much affect us, as the slight benefactions of every ordinary friend; if it cannot so much recommend him to our regard, as to rescue his word from contemt, and dispose us to receive impressions from it; (especially when his very speaking is a new act of his kindness, and design'd to our greatest advantage.)

13. BUT if all he has done and suffer'd for us cannot obtain him so much from us, we must surely confess, our disingenuity is as superlative as his love. For in this instance we have no plea for our selves. The discourses of men tis true may sometime be so weak and irrational, that tho kindness may suggest pity, it cannot reverence; But this can never happen in God, whose wisdom is as infinite as his love. He talks not at our vain rate who

C   often

often talk only for talkings fake; but his words are directed to the moft important ends and addreft in fuch a manner as befits him in whom are all the treafures of wifdom and knowledg, *Col.* 2. And this is our third confideration, the wifdom of the Speaker.

14. How attractive a thing Wifdom is, we may obferve in the inftance of *the Queen of Sheba,* who *came from the utmoft parts of the earth,* as Chrift faies Mat. 12. 42. *to hear the Wifdom of Solomon.* And the like is noted of the Greek Sages, that they were addreft to from all parts, by perfons of all ranks and qualities, to hear their Lectures. And indeed the rational nature of man do's by a kind of fympathetick motion clofe with whatever hath the ftamp of reafon upon it. But alas, what is the profoundeft wifdom of men, compar'd with that of God? He is the effential reafon; and all that man can pretend to is but an emanation from him; a ray of his Sun, a drop of his Ocean: which as he gives, fo he can alfo take away. He can infatuate the moft fubtil defigners; And (as he faies of himfelf) *makes the diviners mad: turns the wife men back, and makes their wifdom foolifhnefs,* Efay 44. 25.

15. How impious a folly is it then in us, to Idolize human Wifdom with all its imperfections, and defpife the divine? yet this every man is guilty of, who is not attracted to the
ftudy

study of sacred Writ by the supereminent wisdom of it's Author. For such men must either affirm that God has not such a supereminency, or that, tho he have in himself, he hath not exerted it in this writing: The former is down-right blasphemy; and truly the latter is the same, a little varied. For that any thing, but what is exactly wise can proceed from infinite wisdom, is too absurd for any man to imagine. And therefore he that charges Gods Word with defect of wisdom, must interpretatively charge God so too. For tho 'tis true, a wise man may sometimes speak foolishly; yet that happens through that mixture of ignorance, or passion which is in the most knowing of mortals: but in God, who is a pure act, and essential wisdom, that is an impossible supposition.

16. N A Y, indeed it were to tax him of folly beyond what is incident to any sensible man; who will still proportion his instruments to the work he designs. Should we not conclude him mad, that should attemt to fell a mighty Oak with a Pen-knife, or stop a Torrent with a wisp of Straw? And sure their conceptions are not much more reverend of God, who can suppose that a writing design'd by him for such important ends, as the *making men wise unto salvation,* 2 Tim. 3. 15. *the casting down all that exalts it self against the obedience of Christ,* 2 Cor. 10. 5. should it self be foolish

and

and weak : or that he should give it those great attributes of being *sharper than a two-edged sword, piercing even to the dividing a sunder of soul and spirit, of the joints and marrow*, Heb. 4. 14. if its discourses were so flat and insipid as some in this profane Age would represent them.

17. 'T1s true indeed, 'tis not, as the Apostle speaks the *wisdom of this world*, 1 Cor. 2. 6. The Scripture teaches us not the arts of undermining governments, defrauding and circumventing our brethren ; but it teaches us that which would tend much more even to our temporal felicity ; and as reason promts us to aspire to happiness, so it must acknowledg that is the highest wisdom which teaches us to attain it.

18. And as the Holy Scripture is thus recommended to us by the wisdom of its Author; so in the last place is it by his truth, without which the other might rather raise our jealousy than our reverence. For wisdom without sincerity degenerates into serpentine guile; and we rather fear to be ensnar'd than hope to be advantag'd by it. The most subtil addresses, and most cogent arguments prevail not upon us, where we suspect some insidious design. But where wisdom and fidelity meet in the same person, we do not only attend, but confide in his counsels. And this qualification is most eminently in God. *Th children*

children of men are deceitfull upon the weights,
Pfal. 62. 9. Much guile often lurks indifcer-
nably under the faireſt appearances : but Gods
veracity is as eſſentially himſelf, as his wiſdom, and he can no more deceive us, than he
can be deceiv'd himſelf. *He is not man that he*
ſhould lie, Num. 23. 19. He defigns not (as
men often do) to ſport himſelf with our credulity; and raiſe hopes which he never means
to ſatisfy : *he ſaies not to the ſeed of* Jacob, *ſeek*
ye me in vain, Ex. 45. 19. but all his *promiſes*
are yea and Amen, 2 Cor. 1. 20. He is perfectly ſincere in all the propoſals he makes in his
word: which is a moſt rational motive for
us to advert to it, not only with reverence but
love.

19. A N D now when all theſe motives are
thus combined; the authority, the kindneſs,
the wiſdom, the veracity of the ſpeaker, what
can be requir'd more to render his words of
weight with us? If this four-fold cord will
not draw us, we have ſure the ſtrength, not of
men, but of that Legion we read of in the
Goſpel, *Mat.* 5. 1. For theſe are ſo much the
cords of man, ſo adapted to our natures,
nay to our conſtant uſage in other things,
that we muſt put off much of our humanity,
diſclaim the common meaſures of mankind,
if we be not attracted by them. For I dare
appeal to the breaſt of any ſober, induſtrious
man, whether in caſe a perſon, who he were
sure

sure had all the fore-mention'd qualifications, should recommend to him some rules as infallible for the certain doubling, or trebling his estate, he would not think them worth the pursuing; nay, whether he would not plod and study on them, till he comprehended the whole Art. And shall we then when God, in whom all those qualifications are united, and that in their utmost transcendencies, shall we, I say, think him below our regard, when he proposes the improving our interests, not by the scanty proportions of two or three; but in such as he intimated to *Abraham,* when he shew'd him the Stars, as the representative of his numerous off-spring, *Gen.* 5. 15. when he teaches us that highest, and yet most certain Alchimy, of refining and multiplying our enjoyments, and then perpetuating them?

20. ALL this God do's in Scripture; and we must be stupidly improvident, if we will take no advantage by it. It was once the complaint of Christ to the Jews, *I am come in my Fathers name, and ye receive me not: if another shall come in his own name, him ye will receive,* Jo. 5. 43. And what was said by him the eternal essential Word, is no less applicable to the written; which coming in the name, and upon the message of God, is despis'd and slighted, and every the lightest composure of men preferr'd before it. As if that signature

of

of Dignity it carries, ferved rather as a Brand to ftigmatize and defame, than adorn and recommend it. A contemt which ftrikes immediatly at God himfelf, whofe refentments of it, tho for the prefent fuppreft by his long-fuffering, will at laft break out upon all who perfevere fo to affront him, in a *judgment worthy of God,* Wif. 12. 26.

21. B u t after all that has bin faid, I forefee fome may fay, that I have all this while but beaten the air, have built upon a principle which fome flatly deny, others doubt of, and have run away with a fuppofition that the Bible is of divine Original, without any attemt of proof. To fuch as thefe I might juftly enough object the extreme hard meafure they offer to Divinity above all other Sciences. For in thofe, they ftill allow fome fundamental maxims, which are prefuppofed without proof; but in this they admit of no *Poftulata,* no granted principle on which to fuperftruct. If the fame rigor fhould be extended to fecular cafes, what a damp would it ftrike upon commerce ? For example, a man expects fair dealing from his neighbor, upon the ftrength of thofe common notions of Juftice he prefumes writ in all mens hearts: but according to this meafure, he muft firft prove to every man he deals with, that fuch notions there are, and that they are obligatory: that the wares expos'd to fale are his own; that dominion

nion is not founded on grace, or that he is in
that ftate, and fo has a property to confer upon another; that the perfon dealt with, paies
a juft price; do's it in good mony; and that it
is his own, or that he is in the ftate of grace;
or needs not be fo, to juftify his purchafe:
and at this rate the Market will be as full of
nice queftions as the Schools.   But becaufe
complaints and retortions are the common
refuge of caufes that want better Arguments,
I fhall not infift here; but proceed to a defence of the queftion'd Affertion, that the
Bible is the Word of God.

22. In which I fhall proceed by thefe degrees.   Firft, I fhall lay down the plain
grounds upon which Chriftians believe it.
Secondly, I fhall compare thofe with thofe of
lefs credibility which have generally fatisfied
mankind in other things of the like nature.
And thirdly, I fhall confider whether thofe
who are diffatisfied with thofe grounds, would
not be equally fo with any other way of atteftation.

23. Before I enter upon the firft of thefe,
I defire it may be confider'd, that matters of fact
are not capable of fuch rigorous demonftrative
evidences, as mathematical propofitions are.
To render a thing fit for rational belief, there
is no more requir'd, but that the motives for it
do over poife thofe againft it; and in that degree they do fo, fo is the belief ftronger or
weaker.   24. Now

24. Now the motives of our belief in the present case, are such as are extrinsic, or intrinsic to the Scriptures; of which the extrinsic are first, and preparative to the other; and indeed all that can reasonably be insisted on to a gain-saier, who must be suppos'd no competent judg of the latter. But as to the former, I shall adventure to say, that the divine Original of the Scripture hath as great grounds of credibility as can be expected in any thing of this kind. For whether God inspir'd the Pen-men of Holy Writ, is matter of fact, and being so, is capable of no other external evidence but that of testimony: and that matter of fact being also in point of time so remote from us, can be judg'd of only by a series of Testimonies deriv'd from that Age wherein the Scriptures were written, to this: and the more credible the testifiers, and the more universal the Testimony; so much the more convincing are they to all considering men.

25. And this attestation the Scripture hath in the highest circumstances, it having bin witnefs'd to in all Ages, and in those Ages by all persons that could be presum'd to know any thing of it. Thus the Old Testament was own'd by the whole Nation of the Jews, as the writings of men inspir'd by God, and that with such evidence of their miffion, as abundantly satisfied those of that Age, of their

D
being

being so inspir'd; and they deriv'd those Writings with that attestation to their posterity. Now that those of the first Ages were not deceiv'd, is as morally certain as any thing can be suppos'd. For in the first part of the Bible is contain'd the history of those miracles wherewith God rescued that people out of *Egypt*, and instated them in *Canaan*. Now if they who liv'd at that time, knew that such miracles were never done, 'tis impossible they could receive an evident Fable as an inspir'd truth. No single person, much less a whole Nation can be suppos'd so stupid. But if indeed they were eye-witnesses of those miracles, they might with very good reason conclude, that the same *Moses* who was by God impower'd to work them, was so also for the relating them; as also all those precedent events from the Creation down to that time, which are recorded by him.

26. So also for the preceptive parts of those Books, those that saw those formidable solemnities, with which they were first publish'd, had sure little temtation to doubt that they were the dictates of God, when written. Now if they could not be deceiv'd themselves, 'tis yet less imaginable that they should conspire to impose a cheat upon their posterities; nor indeed were the Jews of so easy a credulity, that 'tis at all probable the succeeding Generations would have bin so impos'd
on:

on : their humor was ftubborn enough, and the precepts of their Law fevere and burden-fome enough to have temted them to have caft off the yoak, had it not bin bound upon them by irrefiftable convictions of its coming from God. But befides this Tradition of their Elders, they had the advantage of living under a Theocracy, the immediate guidance of God; Prophets daily rais'd up among them, to fore-tell events, to admonifh them of their duty, and reprove their back-flidings: yet even thefe gave the deference to the written Word; nay, made it the teft by which to try true infpirations from falfe : *To the Law and to the Teftimony ; if they fpeak not according to it, there is no light in them,* Efay 8. 20. So that the veneration which they had before acquir'd, was ftill anew excited by frefh infpirations, which both attefted the old, and became new parts of their Canon.

27. Nor could it be efteem'd a fmall confirmation to the Scriptures, to find in fucceeding Ages the fignal accomplifhments of thofe prophecies which were long before regiftred in thofe Books; for nothing lefs than divine Power and Wifdom could foretell, and alfo verify them. Upon thefe grounds the Jews univerfally thro all fucceffions receiv'd the Books of the Old Teftament as divine Oracles, and lookt upon them as the greateft truft that could be committed to them :

D 2

and

and accordingly were ſo ſcrupulouſly vigi-
lant in conſerving them, that their Maſo-
rits numbred not only the ſections, but the
very words, nay letters, that no fraud or in-
advertency might corrupt or defalk the leaſt
iota of what they eſteem'd ſo ſacred. A farther teſtimony and ſepiment to which, were
the Samaritan, Chaldee, and Greek verſions:
which being made uſe of in the Synagogues of
Jews, in their diſperſions, and the Samaritans
at *Sichem*, could not at thoſe diſtances receive
an uniform alteration, and any other would
be of no effect. Add to this, that the Original exemplar of the Law, was laid up in the
Sanctuary, that the Prince was to have a Copy of it allwaies by him, and tranſcribe it with
his own hand; that every Jew was to make
it his conſtant diſcourſe and méditation,
teach it his Children, and wear part of it upon his hands and forehead. And now ſure
'tis impoſſible to imagin any matter of fact
to be more carefully deduced, or irrefraga-
bly teſtified, nor any thing believ'd upon
ſtronger evidence.

28. THAT all this is true in reference to
the Jews, that they did thus own theſe Writings as divine, appears not only by the Records of paſt Ages, but by the Jews of the preſent, who ſtill own them, and cannot be ſu-
ſpected of combination with the Chriſtians.
And if theſe were reaſonable grounds of conviction

viction to the Jews, (as he muft be moft abfurdly fceptical that fhall deny) they muft be fo to Chriftians alfo; who derive them from them: and that with this farther advantage to our Faith, that we fee the clear completion of thofe Evangelical prophecies which remain'd dark to them, and confequently have a farther Argument to confirm us, that the Scriptures of the Old Teftament are certainly divine.

29. THE New has alfo the like means of probation: which as it is a collection of the doctrin taught by Chrift and his Apoftles, muft if truly related be acknowledged no lefs divine than what they orally deliver'd. So that they who doubt its being divine, muft either deny what Chrift and his Apoftles preacht to be fo; or elfe diftruft the fidelity of the relation: The former ftrikes at the whole Chriftian Faith; which if only of men, muft not only be fallible, but is actually a deceit, whilft it pretends to be of God, and is not. To fuch Objectors we have to oppofe thofe ftupendious miracles with which the Gofpel was attefted; fuch as demonftrated a more than human efficacy. And that God fhould lend his omnipotence to abet the falfe pretentions of men, is a conceit too unworthy even for the worft of men to entertain.

30. 'TIS true, there have bin by God permitted

mitted lying miracles, as well as true ones
have bin done by him ; such as were those of
the Magicians in *Egypt*, in opposition to the
other of *Moses* ; but then the difference between both was so conspicuous, that he must
be more partial and disingenuous, than even
those Magicians were, who would not acknowledg the disparity, and confess in those
which were truely supernatural, *the finger of
God*, Exod. 8. 19.   Therefore both in the Old
and New Testament it is predicted, that *false
Prophets should arise, and do signs and wonders,*
Deut. 13. 1. Mat. 24. 11. 24. as a trial of their
fidelity who made profession of Religion ;
whether they would prefer the few and trivial
sleights which recommend a deceiver, before those great and numberless miracles
which attested the sacred Oracles deliver'd
to the sons of men by the God of truth. Whether the trick of a *Barchochebas*, to hold fire in
his mouth ; that of *Marcus* the Heretick, to
make the Wine of the Holy Sacrament appear bloud ; or that of *Mahomet*, to bring a
Pidgeon to his ear, ought to be put in balance against all the Miracles wrought by
Moses, our Savior, or his Apostles.   And in a
word ; whether the silly stories which *Iambli-
chus* solemnly relates of *Pythagoras*, or those
Philostratus tells of *Apollonius Tyaneus*, deserve
to rival those of the Evangelists.   It is a most
just judgment, and accordingly threatned by
Almighty

Almighty God that they who would *not obey*
the truth should believe a lie, 2 Thes. 2. 11.   But
still the Almighty, *where any man* or devil *do's*
proudly, is evidently *above him,* Exod. 18. 11.
will be justified in his sayings, and be clear when
he is judged, Rom. 3. 4.

31. But if men will be Scepticks, and
doubt every thing, they are to know that the
matter call'd into question, is of a nature that
admits but two waies of solution; probability,
and testimony.   First for probability, let it be
consider'd, who were the first promulgers of
Christs Miracles.   In his life time they were
either the patients on whom his Miracles were
wrought, or the common people, that were
spectators: the former, as they could not be
deceiv'd themselves, but must needs know
whether they were cur'd or no; so what Imaginable design could they have to deceive o-
thers? Many indeed have pretended impotency as a motive of compassion; but what could
they gain by owning a cure they had not?
As for the Spectators, as their multitude adds
to their credibility; (it being morally impossible that so many should at once be delu-
ded in a matter so obvious to their senses) so
do's it also acquit them from fraud and combination.   Cheats and forgeries are allwaies
hatcht in the dark, in close Cabals, and private Juncto's.   That five thousand men at one
time, and four thousand at another, should
conspire

conspire to say, that they were miraculously
fed, when they were not ; and all prove true
to the fiction, and not betray it, is a thing as
irrational to be suppos'd, as impossible to be
parallel'd.

32. BESIDES, admit it possible that so many
could have join'd in the deceit, yet what
imaginable end could they have in it ? Had
their lie bin subservient to the designs of some
potent Prince that might have rewarded it,
there had bin some temtation : but what could
they expect from the reputed son of a Carpenter, who had not himself where to lay his
head ? Nay, who disclaim'd all secular power;
convei'd himself away from their importunities, when they would have forc'd him to be
a King : And consequently, could not be
lookt on as one that would head a Sedition,
or attemt to raise himself to a capacity of rewarding his Abettors. Upon all these considerations, there appears not the least shadow
of probability , that either those particular
persons who publish'd the cures they had received, or those multitudes who were witnesses
and divulgers of those, or his other miracles,
could do it upon any sinister design, or indeed
upon any other motive but gratitude and admiration.

33. IN the next place, if we come to those
miracles which succeeded Chrifts death, those
moft important, and convincing of his Refur-

surrection and Ascension, and observe who were the divulgers of those, we shall find them very unlikely to be men of design; a set of illiterate men, taken from the Fisher-Boats, and other mean occupations: and such as needed a miracle as great as any of those they were to assert (the descent of the Holy Ghost) to fit them for their office. What alas could they drive at, or how could they hope that their testimony could be received, so much against the humor and interest of the present Rulers; unless they were assur'd not only of the truth of the things, but also of some supernatural aids to back and fortify them? Accordingly we find, that till they had receiv'd those; till by the descent of the Holy Ghost they were *endued with power from on high*, Luk. 24. 49. they never attemted the discovery of what they had seen: but rather hid themselves, kept all their assemblies in privacy and concealment, *for fear of the Jews*, Jo. 20. 19. and so were far enough from projecting any thing besides their own safety. Afterwards, when they began to preach, they had early essays, what their secular advantages would be by it; threatnings and revilings, scourgings and imprisonments, *Act*. 4. 20. 5. 18, 40. And can it be imagined, that men who a little before had shewed themselves so little in love with suffering, that none of them durst stick to their Master at his apprehension, but

E   one

one forſwore, and all forſook him ; can it, I ſay, be imagin'd that theſe men ſhould be ſo much in love with their own Fable, as to venture all ſorts of perſecution for the propagating it ? Or if they could, let us in the next place conſider what probability there could be of ſucceſs.

34. THEIR preaching amounted to no leſs than the Deifying of one, whom both their Roman and Jewiſh Rulers, nay, the generality of the people had executed as a malefactor : ſo that they were all engag'd, in defence of their own Act, to ſift their teſtimony with all the rigor that conſcious jealouſy could ſuggeſt. And where were ſo many concern'd inquiſitors, there was very little hope for a forgery to paſs. Beſides the avow'd diſpleaſure of their Governors made it a hazardous thing to own a belief of what they aſſerted. Thoſe that adher'd to them could not but know, that at the ſame time they muſt eſpouſe their dangers and ſufferings. And men uſe not to incur certain miſchiefs, upon doubtful and ſuſpicious grounds.

35. YET further, their doctrin was deſign'd to an end to which their Auditors could not but have the greateſt reluctancy : they were to ſtruggle with that rooted prepoſſeſſion which the Jews had for the Moſaical Law, which their Goſpel out-dated ; and the Gentiles for the Rites and Religion of their Anceſtors ;

ceftors; and, which was harder than either, with the corruptions and vices of both : to plant humility and internal fanctity, fo contrary to that ceremonial holinefs, upon which the Jews fo valued themfelves, and defpis'd others : and Temperance, Juftice, and Purity, fo contrary to the practice, nay, even the religion of the Heathen : and to attemt all this with no other allurement, no other promife of recompence but what they muft attend in another world, and pafs too through reproches and afflictions, torments and death ; Thefe were all fuch invincible prejudices, as they could never hope to break thorow with a lie ; nay, which they could not have encounter'd even with every common truth, but only with that, which being divine, brought its aids with it ; without which 'twas utterly impoffible for all the skill or oratory of men to overcome fuch difadvantages.

36. AND yet with all thefe did thefe rude inartificial men conteft, and that with fignal fuccefs : no lefs than three thoufand Profelytes made by Saint *Peters* firft Sermon ; and that in *Jerufalem*, the Scene where all was acted, and confequently where 'twas the moft impoffible to impofe a forgery. And at the like miraculous rate they went on, till as the Pharifees themfelves complain, they had *filled Jerufalem with their doctrin*, Acts. 5. 28. nor did *Judea* fet bounds to them ; *their found went*

out

out into all Nations, Rom. 10. 18. and their
doctrin ſpread it ſelf through all the Gentile
world.

37. AND ſure ſo wonderful an event, ſo
contrary to all human meaſures, do's ſufficiently evince there was more than man in it.
Nothing but the ſame creative Power that
produc'd light out of darkneſs, could bring
forth effects ſo much above the proportion of
the cauſe. Had theſe weak inſtruments acted
only by their natural powers, nothing of this
had bin atchiev'd. Alas could theſe poor rude
men learn all Languages within the ſpace of
fifty days, which would take up almoſt as many years of the moſt induſtrious Student, and
yet had they not bin able to ſpeak them, they
could never have divulg'd the Goſpel to the
ſeveral Nations, nor ſo effectually have convinc'd the by-ſtanders, *Act.* 2. that they acted
by a higher impulſe. And to convince the
world they did ſo, they repeated their Maſters
miracles as well as his doctrin ; heal'd the
ſick, caſt out devils, rais'd the dead. And
where God communicated ſo much of his
power, we may reaſonably conclude he did
it to promote his own work, not the work of
the devil, as it muſt have bin if this whole
Scene were a lie.

38. WHEN all this is weigh'd, I preſume
there will remain little ground to ſuſpect,
that the firſt planters of Chriſtian Faith had
                                                    any

any other defign than what they avowed, *viz.* the bringing men to holinefs here, and falvation hereafter. The fufpicion therefore, if any, muft reft upon latter times; and accordingly fome are willing to perfwade themfelves and others, that the whole Scheme of our Religion is but a lately devis'd Fable to keep the world in awe, whereof Princes have made fome ufe, but Clergy-men more; and that Chrift and his Apoftles are only actors whom themfelves have conjured up upon the ftage to purfue their plot.

39. I N anfwer to this bold, this blafphemous fuggeftion, I fhould firft defire thefe furmifers to point out the time when, and the perfons who began this defign; to tell us exactly whence they date this politick Religion, as they are pleas'd to fuppofe it. If they cannot, they are manifeftly unjuft to reject our account of it when they can give none themfelves; and fail very much of that rigid demonftration they require from others. That there is fuch a profeffion as Chriftianity in the world, is yet (God be bleft) undeniable; (though at the rate it has of late declin'd, God knows how long it will be fo :) we fay it came by Chrift, and his Apoftles, and that it is attefted by an uninterrupted teftimony of all the intervening Ages, the fuffrage of all Chriftian Churches from that day to this. And fure they who embraced the doctrin, are the

moft

moft competent witneffes from whence they received it.

40. Y E T left they fhould be all thought parties to the defign, and their witnefs excepted againft, it has pleas'd God to give us collateral affurances, and make both Jewifh and Gentile Writers give teftimony to the Antiquity of Chriftianity. *Jofephus* do's this, lib. 20. chap. 8. and lib. 18. chap. 4. where, after he has given an account of the crucifixion of Chrift exactly agreeing with the Evangelifts; he concludes, *And to this day the Chriftian people, who of him borrow their name, ceafe not to increafe.* I add not the perfonal elogium which he gives of our Savior; becaufe fome are fo hardy to controul it : alfo, I pafs by what *Philo* mentions of the religious in *Egypt*, becaufe feveral Learned men refer it to the *Effens*, a Sect among the Jews, or fome other. There is no doubt of what *Tacitus* and other Roman Hiftorians fpeak of Chrift as the Author of the Chriftian doctrin ; which it had bin impoffible for him to have done, if there had then bin no fuch doctrin, or if Chrift had not bin known as the Founder of it. So afterward *Plinie* gives the Emperor *Trajan* an account both of the manners, and multitude of the Chriftians ; and makes of the innocence of the one, and the greatnefs of the other, an Argument to flacken the perfecution againft them. Nay, the very bloody Edicts

of

of the perfecuting Emperors, & the fcoffs and reproches of *Celfus, Porphyry, Lucian,* and other profane oppofers of this Doctrin, do undeniably affert its being. By all which it appears, that Chriftianity had in thofe Ages not only a being, but had alfo obtain'd mightily in the world, and drawn in vaft numbers to its profeffion : and vaft indeed they muft needs be, to furnifh out that whole Army of Martyrs, of which profane, as well as Ecclefiaftick writers fpeak. And if all this be not fufficient to evince that Chriftianity ftole not clancularly into the world, but took its rife from thofe times and perfons it pretends, we muft renounce all faith of teftimony, and not believe an inch farther than we fee.

41. I fuppofe I need,fay no more to fhew that the Gofpel, and all thofe portentous miracles which attefted it, were no forgeries, or ftratagems of men. I come now to that doubt which more immediatly concerns the Holy Scripture, *viz.* whether all thofe tranfactions be fo faithfully related there, that we may believe them to have bin dictated by the fpirit of God. Now for this, the procefs need be but fhort, if we confider who were the penmen of the New Teftament ; even for the moft part of the Apoftles themfelves : *Matthew,* and *John* who wrote two of the Gofpels were certainly fo : and *Mark,* as all the Ancients aver, was but the Amanuenfis to Saint

Peter,

Peter, who dictated that Gospel.   Saint *Luke*
indeed comes not under this first rank of A-
postles ; yet is by some affirm'd to be one of the
seventy Disciples :   however an Apostolical
person 'tis certain he was, and it was no wonder for such to be inspir'd.   For in those first
Ages of the Church men acted more by immediate inflation of the Spirit than since.   And
accordingly we find *Stephen,* tho but a Deacon,
had the power of miracles ; and preacht as divinely as the prime Apostles, *Act.* 7.   And the
gift of the Holy Ghost was then a usual concomitant of conversion, as appears in the Story
of *Cornelius,* Acts 10. 45, 46.   Besides, Saint
Luke was a constant attendant on Saint *Paul*
(who derived the Faith *not from man, but by the*
immediate *revelation of Jesus Christ,* as himself
professes, *Gal.* 1. 12.) and is by some said to
have wrote by dictate from him, as *Mark*
did from Saint *Peter.*   Then as to the Epistles
they all bear the names of Apostles, except
that to the Hebrews, which yet is upon very
good grounds presum'd to be Saint *Paul's.*
Now these were the persons commissionated
by Christ to preach the Christian doctrin, and
were signally assisted in the discharge of that
office ; so that as he tells them, it was *not they,*
who speak, but the spirit of the Father that spake
in them, Mat. 13. 11.   And if they spake by
divine inspiration, there can be no question
that they wrote so also.   Nay, indeed of the
two,

two, it feems more neceffary they fhould do
the latter. For had they err'd in any thing
they orally deliver'd, they might have retra-
&ed and cured the mifchief: but thefe Books
being defign'd as a ftanding immutable rule
of Faith and Manners to all fucceffions, any
errour in them would have bin irreparable, and
have entail'd it felf upon pofterity: which
agreed neither with the truth, nor goodnefs
of God to permit.

42. N o w that thefe Books were indeed
writ by them whofe names they bear, we have
as much affurance as 'tis poffible to have of
any thing of that nature, and that diftance
of time from us. For however fome of them
may have bin controverted, yet the greateft
part have admitted no difpute; whofe do-
&rines agreeing exactly with the others, give
teftimony to them. And to the bulk of thofe
writings, it is notorious that the firft Chriftians receiv'd them from the Apoftles, and fo
tranfmitted them to the enfuing Ages, which
receiv'd them with the like efteem and veneration. *They cannot be corrupted,* fays Saint
Auftin in the thirty fecond Book againft *Fau-
ftus* the Manich. c. 16. *becaufe they are and
have been in the hands of all Chriftians. And who-
foever fhould firft attemt an alteration, he would
be confuted by the infpection of other ancienter
copies. Befides, the Scriptures are not in fome one
Language, but tranflated into many: fo that the*

F   *faults*

faults of one Book would be corrected by others more
ancient, or in a different Tongue.

43. AND how much the body of Christians
were in earnest concern'd to take care in this
matter, appears by very costly evidences; multitudes of them choosing rather to part with
their lives than their Bibles. And indeed 'tis
a sufficient proof, that their reverence of that
Book was very avowed and manifest; when
their Heathen persecutors made that one part
of their persecution. So that as wherever
the Christian Faith was receiv'd, this Book
was also, under the notion we now plead for,
viz. as the writings of men inspir'd by God:
so it was also contended for even unto death;
and to part with the Bible was to renounce
the Faith. And now, after such a cloud of testimonies, we may sure take up that (ill applyed)
saying of the High Priest, Matt. 26. 65. *what*
further need have we of witnesses.

44. YET besides these, another sort of witnesses there are, I mean those intrinsic evidences which arise out of the Scripture it self;
but of these I think not proper here to insist,
partly because the subject will be in a great
degree coincident with that of the second
general consideration; and partly because
these can be argumentative to none who are
not qualified to discern them. Let those
who doubt the divine Original of Scripture,
well digest the former grounds which are
                                           within

within the verge of reason; and when by those they are brought to read it with due reverence, they will not want Arguments from the Scripture it self to confirm their veneration of it.

45. In the mean time, to evince how proper the former discourse is to found a rational belief that the Scripture is the word of God; I shall compare it with those measures of credibility upon which all humane transactions move, and upon which men trust their greatest concerns without diffidence or dispute.

46. That we must in many things trust the report of others, is so necessary, that without it humane society cannot subsist. What a multitude of subjects are there in the world, who never saw their Prince, nor were at the making of any Law? if all these should deny their obedience, because they have it only by hear-say; there is such a man, and such Laws, what would become of Government? So also for property, if nothing of testimony may be admitted, how shall any man prove his right to any thing? All pleas must be decided by the sword, and we shall fall into that state (which some have fancied the primitive) of universal hostility. In like manner for traffick and commerce; how should any Merchant first attempt a trade to any foreign part of the world, if he did not be-

lieve

lieve that such a place there was? and how could he believe that, but upon the credit of those who have bin there? Nay, indeed how could any man first attemt to go but to the next Market Town, if he did not from the report of others, conclude that such a one there was? so that if this universal diffidence should prevail, every man should be a kind of *Plantagnus*, fixt to the soil he first sprung up in. The absurdities are indeed so infinite, and so obvious, that I need not dilate upon them.

47. BUT it will perhaps be said, that in things that are told us by our contemporaries, and that relate to our own time, men will be less apt to deceive us, because they know 'tis in our power to examine and discover the truth. To this I might say, that in many instances it would scarce quit cost to do so, and the inconveniences of tryal would exceed those of belief. But I shall willingly admit this probable argument, and only desire it may be applied to our main question, by considering whether the primitive Christians who receiv'd the Scripture as divine, had not the same security of not being deceiv'd, who had as great opportunities of examining, and the greatest concern of doing it throughly, since they were to engage, not only their futures hopes in another world, but (that which to nature is much more sensible)

all

all their prefent enjoyments, and even life it felf upon the truth of it.

48. B u t becaufe it muft be confeft that we who are fo many Ages remov'd from them, have not their means of affurance; let us in the next place confider, whether an affent to thofe teftimonies they have left behind them, be not warranted by the common practice of mankind in other cafes. Who is there that queftions there was fuch a man as *William* the Conqueror in this Ifland? Or, to lay the Scene farther, who doubts there was an *Alexander*, a *Julius Cefar*, an *Auguftus*? Now what have we to found this confidence on befides the Faith of Hiftory? And I prefume even thofe who exact the fevereft demonftrations for Ecclefiaftick ftory, would think him a very impertinent Sceptick that fhould do the like in thefe. So alfo, as to the Authors of Books; who difputes whether *Homer* writ the Iliads, or *Virgil* the Æneids, or *Cefar* the Commentaries, that pafs under their names? yet none of thefe have been attefted in any degree like the Scripture. 'Tis faid indeed, that *Cefar* ventured his own life to fave his Commentaries, imploying one hand to hold thofe above the water, when it fhould have affifted him in fwiming. But whoever laid down their lives in attestation of that, or any humane compofure, as multitudes of men have done for the Bible?

49. B u t

49. BUT perhaps 'twill be said, that the small concern men have, who wrote thefe, or other the like Books, inclines them to acquiefce in the common opinion. To this I muſt fay, that many things inconfiderable to mankind have oft bin very laborioufly difcuſt, as appears by many unedifying Volumes, both of Philofophers and School-men. But whatever may be faid in this inſtance, 'tis manifeſt there are others, wherein mens real and greateſt intereſts are intruſted to the teſtimonies of former Ages. For example, a man poffeffes an eftate which was bought by his great Grandfather, or perhaps elder Progenitor: he charily preferves that deed of purchafe, and never looks for farther fecurity of his title: yet alas, at the rate that men objeċt againſt the Bible, what numberlefs Cavils might be rais'd againſt fuch a deed? How fhall it be known that there was fuch a man as either Seller or Purchafer? if by the witneffes they are as lyable to doubt as the other; it being as eafie to forge the atteſtation as the main writing: and yet notwithſtanding all thefe poffible deceits, nothing but a pofitive proof of forgery can invalidate this deed. Let but the Scripture have the fame meafure, be allowed to ſtand in force, to be what it pretends to be, till the contrary be (not by furmifes and poffible conjeċtures) but by evident proof evinc'd; and its greateſt Advocates will ask no more.

50. A

50. A like inftance may be given in publick concerns: the immunities and rights of any Nation, particularly here of our *Magna Charta*, granted many Ages fince, and depofited among the publick Records: to make this fignify any thing, it muft be taken for granted, that this was without falfification preferved to our times; yet how eafy were it to fuggeft that in fo long a fucceffion of its keepers, fome may have bin prevail'd on by the influence of Princes to abridge and curtail its conceffions; others by a prevailing faction of the people to amplify and extend it? Nay, if men were as great Soepticks in Law, as they are in Divinity, they might exact demonftrations that the whole thing were not a forgery. Yet, for all thefe poffible furmifes, we ftill build upon it, and fhould think he argued very fallacioufly, that fhould go to evacuate it, upon the force of fuch remote fuppofitions.

51. Now I defire it may be confider'd whether our fecurity concerning the holy Scripture be not as great, nay, greater than it can be of this. For firft, this is a concern only of a particular Nation, and fo can expect no foreign atteftation; and fecondly, it has all along refted on the fidelity of its keepers; which has bin either a fingle perfon, or at beft fome fmall number at a time; whereas the Scriptures have bin witnefs'd to by perfons of all Nations, and thofe not fingle, but collective

&ive Bodies and Societies, even as many as there have bin Chriftian Churches throughout the world. And the fame that are its Atteftors have bin its Guardians alfo, and by their multitudes made it a very difficult, if not an impoffible thing to falfify it in any confiderable degree; it being not imaginable, as I fhew'd before from St. *Auftin,* all Churches fhould combine to do it: and if they did not, the fraud could not pafs undete&ed: and if no eminent change could happen, much lefs could any new, any counterfeit Gofpel be obtruded, after innumerable Copies of the firft had bin tranflated into almoft all Languages, and difperft throughout the world.

52. THE Imperial Law compil'd by *Juftinian,* was foon after his death, by reafon of the inroads of the *Goths,* and other barbarous Nations, utterly loft in the Weftern world; and fcarce once heard of for the fpace of five hundred years, and then came cafually to be retriv'd upon the taking of *Amalfis* by the *Pifans,* one fingle copy being found there at the plundering of the City. And the whole credit of thofe Pande&s, which have ever fince govern'd the Weftern world, depends in a manner on that fingle Book, formerly call'd the *Pifan;* and now, after that *Pifa* was taken by the *Florentines,* the *Florentine* Copy. But notwithftanding this, the body of the Civil Law obtains; and no man thinks it reafonable

able to queftion its being really what it pretends to be, notwithftanding its fingle, and fo long interrupted derivation. I might draw this parallel thro many other inftances, but thefe may fuffice to fhew, that if the Scripture might find but fo much equity, as to be tried by the common meafures of other things, it would very well pafs the teft.

53. BUT men feem in this cafe (like our late Legiflators) to fet up new extraregular Courts of Juftice, to try thofe whom no ordinary rules will caft, yet their defigns require fhould be condemn'd: And we may conclude, 'tis not the force of reafon, but of prejudice, that makes them fo unequal to themfelves as to rejeĉt the Scripture, when they receive every thing elfe upon far weaker grounds. The bottom of it is, they are refolv'd not to obey its precepts; and therefore think it the fhorteft cut to difavow its autority: for fhould they once own that, they would find themfelves intangled in the moft inextricable dilemma; that of the Pharifees about *John Baptift : If we fay from heaven, he will fay, why then did you not believe him ?* Mat. 21. 25. If they confefs the Scriptures divine, they muft be felf-condemn'd in not obeying them. And truly men that have fuch preingagements to their lufts, that they muft admit nothing that will difturb them; do but prevaricate when they call for greater evidence

G   and

and demonstrations: for those bosom Sophisters will elude the most manifest convictions; and like Juglers, make men disbelieve even their own senses. So that any other waies of evidence will be as disputable with them, as those already offer'd: which is the third thing I proposed to consider.

54. I T has been sometimes seen in popular mutinies, that when blanks have been sent them they could not agree what to ask: and were it imaginable that God should so far court the infidelity of men, as to allow them to make their own demands, to set down what waies of proof would perswade them; I doubt not there are many have obstinacy enough to defeat their own methods, as well as they do now Gods. 'Tis sure there is no ordinary way of conviction left for them to ask, God having already (as hath also bin shew'd) afforded that. They must therefore resort to immediate revelation, expect instant assurances from heaven, that this book we call the Bible is the word of God.

55. M Y first question then is, in what manner this revelation must be made to appear credible to them. The best account we have of the several waies of revelation is from the Jews, to whom God was pleas'd upon new emergencies signally to reveal himself. These were first dreams; secondly, visions; by both which the Prophets received
ved

ved their infpirations. Thirdly, *Urim* and *Thummim*. Fourthly, the *Bath-col* (as they term it) Thunder and voice from Heaven. Let us confider them diftinctly, and fee whether our Sceptical men may not probably find fomewhat to difpute in every one of thefe. And firft for dreams, it is among us fo hard to diftinguifh between thofe that arife from conftitution, prepoffeffion of phancy, diabolical, or divine infufion, that thofe that have the moft critically confider'd them, do rather difference them by their matter, than any certain difcriminating circumftances: and unlefs we had fome infallible way of difcerning, our dependence on them may more probably betray than direct us. 'Tis unqueftionable that ufually phancy has the greateft ftroke in them. And if he that fhould commit himfelf to the guidance of his waking phancy, is not like to be over-wifely govern'd, what can we expect from his fleeping? All this and more may doubtlefs be foberly enough objected againft the validity of our common dreams.

56. BUT admit there were now fuch divine dreams as brought their evidence along with them; yet fure 'tis poffible for prejudic'd men to refift even the cleareft convictions. For do we not fee fome that have made a fhift to extinguifh that natural light, thofe notions which are interwoven into the very frame and conftitution of their minds, that

fo

ſo they may ſin more at eaſe, and without reluctancy? and ſure 'tis as poſſible for them to
cloſe their eies againſt all raies from without
too, to reſiſt revelation as well as inſtinct;
and more likely, by how much a tranſient
cauſe is naturally leſs operative than a per-
manent. An inſtance of this we have in _Ba-
laam_, who being in theſe nightly viſitations
prohibited by God to go to _Balak_; and tho
he knew then what he afterwards ſaies, _Num._
23. 19. that _God was not a man that he ſhould
lie, nor the ſon of man that he ſhould repent_; yet
he would not take God at his firſt word, but
upon a freſh bait to his covetouſneſs, tries a-
gain for an anſwer more indulgent to his intereſt. Beſides, if God ſhould thus reveal himſelf to ſome particular perſons, yet 'tis beyond
all preſident or imagination, that he ſhould
do it to every man; and then how ſhall thoſe
who have theſe dreams, be able to convince
others that they are divine?

57. 'Tis eaſy to gueſs what reception a
man that produces no other autority, would
have in this ludicrous Age: he would certainly be thought rather to want ſleep, than to
have had revelations in it. And if _Jacob_ and
the Patriarchs, who were themſelves acquain-
ted with divine dreams, yet did not believe
Joſephs; any man that ſhould now pretend in
that kind, would be ſure to fall under the
ſame irony that he did, to be entertain'd with
a _be-_

a *behold this dreamer cometh*, Gen. 37. 19.

58. THE second way of revelation by vision was, where the man was wrapt into an extafy, his fpirit for a while fufpended from all fenfible communication with the body, and entertain'd with fupernatural light. In thefe the Prophets faw emblematical reprefentations of future events, receiv'd knowledg of divine Myfteries, and commiffion and ability to difcharge the whole prophetic office. Now fuppofe God fhould now raife us Prophets, and infpire them after this manner; what would the merry men of this time fay to it? Can we think that they who rally upon all that the former Prophets have writ, would look with much reverence on what the new ones fhould fay? Some perhaps would conftrue their raptures to be but like Mahomets Epilepfy; others a fit of frenzy, others perhaps a being *drunk with new wine* Act. 2. 13. but thofe that did the moft foberly confider it, would ftill need a new revelation to atteft the truth of this: there being far more convincing arguments to prove the Scriptures divine, than any man can allege to prove his infpiration to be fo. And 'tis fure a very irrational method, to attemt the clearing of a doubt by fomewhat which is it felf more doubtful.

59. A third way, was by *Urim* and *Thummim*, which Writers tell us was an Oracle refulting from the Letters which were graven
in

in the High Priests Pectoral, to which in all important doubts the Jews of thofe Ages reforted, and receiv'd refponfes; but whether it were by the fuddain prominency, or refplendency of the letters, or by any other way, is not material in this place to enquire: one thing is certain, that the Ephod, and confequently the Pectoral was in the Priests cuftody, and that he had the adminiftration of the whole affair.   Now I refer it to confideration, whether this one circumftance would not (to thofe prejudic'd men I fpeak of) utterly evacuate the credit of the Oracle.   They have taught themfelves to look on Prieft-hood, whether Legal or Evangelical, only as a better name for impofture and cofenage: and they that can accufe the Priests for having kept up a cheat for fo many Ages, muft needs think them fuch omnipotent Juglers, that nothing can be fence againft their Legerdemain: and by confequence, this way of revelation would rather foment their difpleafure at the Ecclefiafticks, than fatisfy their doubts of the Scripture.

60. Lastly, for the fourth way, that of thunder and voice from Heaven, tho that would be a fignal way of conviction to unprejudiced men, yet it would probably have as little effect as the reft upon the others: men that pretend to fuch deep reafoning, would think it childifh to be frighted out of their
opinion

opinion by a clap of Thunder; some philosophical reason shall be found out, to satisfy them that 'tis the effect only of some natural cause, and any the most improbable shall serve turn to supplant the fear of its being a divine testimony to that which they are so unwilling should be true. As for the voice from Heaven, it must either be heard by others, and related to them; or else immediatly by themselves: if the former, 'twill lie under the same prejudice which the Bible already do's, that they have it but by hearsay: and reporters would fall under the reproach either of design or frenzy; that they meant to deceive, or were themselves deceiv'd by their own distemper'd phancy. But if themselves should be Auditors of it; 'tis odds but their bottomless jealousies in divine Matters would suggest a possibility of fraud, tho they knew not how to trace it; nay 'tis more than possible that they will rather disbelieve their own senses, than in this instance take their testimony with all its consequences.

61. Nor is this a wild supposition: for we see it possible for not only single men, but multitudes to disbelieve their senses thro an excess of credulity; witness the doctrine of Transubstantiation. Why may it not then be as possible for others to do the like thro a greater excess of incredulity? Besides mens prepossessions and affections have a strange influence

influence on their Faith: men many times will not suffer themselves to believe the most credible things, if they cross their inclination. How often do we see irregular patients that will not believe any thing that their appetite craves, will do them hurt, tho their Phyficians, nay, their own even senfitive experience atteft it to them? And can we think that a diseas'd mind, gafping with an Hydropick thirft after the pleasures of fin, will ever affent to those premises, whose conclusion will engage to the renouncing them? Will not a luxurious voluptuous person be willing rather to give his ears the lie, to disbelieve what he hears, than permit them more deeply to disoblige his other fenfes, by bringing in those reftraints and mortifications which the Scripture would impose upon them?

62. Thus we see how little probability there is, that any of these waies of revelation would convince these incredulous men. And indeed, those that will not believe upon such inducements as may satisfy men of sober reason, will hardly submit to any other method, according to that Affertion of Father *Abraham, If they hear not* Moses *and the Prophets, neither will they be perfwaded, tho one rose from the dead,* Luk. 16. 31. Now at this rate of infidelity, what way will they leave God to manifeft any thing convincingly to the world? which is to put him under an impotency

tency greater than adheres to humanity: for we men have power to communicate our minds to others, tell whetherto we own such or such a thing to which we are intitled; and we can satisfy our Auditors that it is indeed we that speak of them: but if every method God uses, do's rather increase than satisfy mens doubts, all intercourse between God and man is intercepted; and he must do that of necessity, which *Epicurus* phancied he did of his choice; *viz.* keep himself unconcern'd in the affairs of mortals, as having no way of communicating with them. Nay (what is yet, if possible, more absurd) he must be suppos'd to have put the works of his Creation out of his own reach, to have given men discoursive faculties, and left himself no way of address to them.

63. THESE inferences how horridly soever they sound, yet I see not how they can be disclaim'd by those, who are unsatisfied with all those waies by which God hath hitherto reveal'd himself to the world. For can it be imagin'd, that God who created man a reasonable creature, that himself might be glorified in his free and rational obedience: (when all other creatures obey upon impulse and instinct) can it, I say, be imagin'd, that he should so remisly pursue his own design, as to let so many Ages pass since the Creation, and never to acquaint mankind with the

H   parti-

particulars wherein that obedience was to be exercis'd. This ſure were ſo diſagreeable to his wiſdom and goodneſs, that it cannot be charg'd upon his will: and conſequently they who own not that he has made any ſuch revelation, muſt tacitly tax him of impotence, that he could not do it. But if any man will ſay he has, and yet rejeƈt all this which both Jews and Chriſtians receive as ſuch, let him produce his teſtimonies for the others, or rather (to retort his own meaſure) his demonſtrations. And then let it appear whether his Scheme of doƈtrin, or ours, will need the greater aid of that eaſy credulity he reproaches us with.

64. I have now gone throw the method I propoſed for evincing the Divine Original of the Scriptures, and ſhall not deſcend to examine thoſe more minute and particular Cavils which profane men make againſt them; the proof of this, virtually ſuperſeding all thoſe. For if it be reaſonable to believe it the Word of God, it muſt be reaſonable alſo to believe it of perfeƈtion proportionable to the Author; and then certainly it muſt be advanc'd beyond all our objeƈtions. For to thoſe who except to the ſtile, the incoherence, the contradiƈtions, or whatever elſe in Scripture; I ſhall only ask this one queſtion, whether it be not much more poſſible that they (who can pretend to be nothing above fallible

lible men) may misjudge, than that the infallible God should dictate any thing justly liable to those charges: I am sure they must depart as much from Reason as Religion, to affirm the contrary. But alas, instead of this implicit submission to Gods Word, men take up explicit prejudices against it; condemn it without ever examining the truth of the allegation. 'Tis certain, that in a writing of such Antiquity, whose original Language has Idioms and Phrases so peculiar, whose Country had customs so differing from the rest of the world; 'tis impossible to judg of it without reference to all those circumstances. Add to this, that the Hebrew has bin a dead Language for well nigh two thousand years, nowhere in common use: nor is there any other ancient Book now extant in it, besides those (yet not all neither,) of the Old Testament.

65. Now of those many who defame Holy Writ, how few are there that have the industry to enquire into those particulars? And when for want of knowledg, some passages seem improper, or perhaps contradictory; the Scripture must bear the blame of their ignorance, and be accus'd as absurd and unintelligible, because themselves are stupid and negligent. It were therefore methinks but a reasonable proposal, that no man should arraign it, till they have used all honest diligence, taken in all probable helps for the un-

derstand-

derstanding it : and if this might be obtain'd,
I believe most of its Accusers would like those
of the woman in the Gospel *Jo.* 8. 9. drop a-
way, as conscious of their own incompeten-
cy : the loudest out-cries that are made a-
gainst it, being commonly of those who fall
upon it only as a fashionable theme of dif-
course, and hope to acquire themselves the
reputation of wits by thus charging God foolishly. But he that would candidly and up-
rightly endeavor to comprehend before he
judges, and to that end industriously use those
means which the providence of God by the
labours of pious men hath afforded him, will
certainly find cause to acquit the Scripture
of those imputations which our bold Criticks
have cast upon it. I do not say that he shall
have all the obscurities of it perfectly clear'd
to him; but he shall have so many of them as
is for his real advantage, and shall discern
such reasons why the rest remain unfathomable, as may make him not only justify, but
celebrate the wisdom of the Author.

66. YET this is to be expected only upon
the fore-mention'd condition, *viz.* that he
come with sincere and honest intentions; for
as for him that comes to the Scripture with
design, and wishes to find matter of cavil and
accusations; there is little doubt but that
spirit of impiety and profaness which sent
him thither, will meet him there as a spirit
of

of delufion, and occecation. That Prince of the Air will caft fuch mifts, raife fuch black vapors; that as the Apoftle fpeaks, *the light of the glorious Gofpel of Chrift fhall not fhine unto him*, 2. Cor. 4. 5. Indeed were fuch a man left only to the natural efficacy of prejudice, that is of it felf fo blinding, fo infatuating a thing, as commonly fortifies againft all conviction. We fee it in all the common inftances of life; mens very fenfes are often enflav'd by it: the prepoffeffion of a ftrong phancy will make the objects of fight or hearing appear quite different from what they are. But in the prefent cafe, when this fhall be added to Satanical illufions, and both left to their operations by Gods withdrawing his illuminating grace, the cafe of fuch a man anfwers that defcription of the Scripture, *They have eies and fee not, ears have they and hear not*, Rom. 11. 8. And that God will fo withdraw his grace, we have all reafon to believe; he having promis'd it only to the meek, to thofe who come with malleable ductile fpirits, to learn, not to deride or cavil. Saint *Peter* tells us, that the *unlearned and unftable wreft the Scripture to their own deftruction*, 2. Pet. 3. 16. And if God permit fuch to do fo, much more will he the proud and malicious.

67. I fay not this, to deter any from the ftudy of Holy Scripture, but only to caution them to bring a due preparation of mind along

long with them; Gods Word being like a generous foveraign medicament, which if fim-
ply and regularly taken, is of the greateſt benefit; but if mixt with poiſon, ſerves only to
make that more fatally operative.   To conclude, he that would have his doubts folv'd
concerning Scripture, let him follow the method our bleſſed Lord has prefcrib'd : Let
him *do the will of God, and then he ſhall know of
the doctrin, whether it be of God,* Jo. 7. 17.   Let
him bring with him a probity of mind, a wil-
lingneſs to aſſent to all convictions he ſhall
there meet with; and then he will find grounds
ſufficient to aſſure him that it is Gods Word,
and conſequently to be receiv'd with all the
ſubmiſſion and reverence, that its being ſo
exacts.

SECT.

SECT. III.

The subject matter treated of in the Holy Scripture, is excellent; as is also its end and design.

WE have hitherto consider'd the holy Scripture only under one notion, as it is the Word of God; we come now to view it in the subject matter of it, the several parts whereof it consists; which are so various and comprehensive, as shews the whole is deriv'd from *him who is all in all* 1 Cor. 15. 28. But that we may not speak only loosely, and at rovers, we will take this excellent frame in pieces, and consider its most eminent parts distinctly. Now the parts of Holy Writ seem to branch themselves into these severals: First, the Historical; secondly, the Prophetick; thirdly, the Doctrinal; fourthly, the Preceptive; fifthly, the Minatory; sixthly, the Promissory. These are the several veins in this rich Mine, in which he who industriously labours, will find the Psalmist was not out in his estimate, when he pronounces them *more to be desir'd than gold, yea, than much fine gold,* Psal. 19. 10.

2. To speak first of the Historical part, the

the things which chiefly recommend a History, are the dignity of the subject, the truth of the relation, and those pleasant or profitable observations which are interwoven with it. And first, for the dignity of the subject, the History of the Bible must be acknowledged to excell all others: those shew the rise and progress of some one people or Empire; this shews us the original of the whole Universe; and particularly of man, for whose use and benefit the whole Creation was design'd. By this mankind is brought into acquaintance with it self; made to know the elements of its constitution, and taught to put a differing value upon that Spirit which was *breath'd into it by God*, Gen. 2. 7. and the flesh whose *foundation is in the dust*, Job. 4. 19. And when this Historical part of Scripture contracts and draws into a narrow channel, when it records the concerns but of one Nation, yet it was that which God had dignified above all the rest of the world, markt it out for his own peculiar; made it the repository of his truth, and the visible stock from whence the Messias should come, in whom *all the Nations of the earth were to be blessed*, Gen. 18. 18. so that in this one people of the Jews, was virtually infolded the highest and most important interests of the whole world; and it must be acknowledg'd, no Story could have a nobler subject to treat of.

3. Se-

3. SECONDLY, as to the truth of the relation, tho to thofe who own it Gods Word there needs no other proof ; yet it wants not human Arguments to confirm it. The moft undoubted fymptom of fincerity in an Hiftorian is impartiality. Now this is very eminent in Scripture writers : they do not record others faults, and baulk their own; but indifferently accufe themfelves as well as others. *Mofes* mentions his own diffidence and unwillingnefs to go on Gods meffage, *Ex.* 4. 13. his provocation of God at the waters of *Meribah*, Num. 20. *Jonah* records his own fullen behaviour towards God, with as great aggravations as any of his enemies could have done. *Peter* in his dictating Saint *Marks* Gofpel, neither omits nor extenuates his fin ; all he feems to fpeak fhort in, is his repentance. Saint *Paul* regifters himfelf as the greateft of finners.

4. AND as they were not indulgent to their own perfonal faults, fo neither did any nearnefs of relation, any refpect of quality bribe them to a concealment : *Mofes* relates the offence of his Sifter *Miriam* in mutining. *Num.* 12. 1. of his Brother *Aaron* in the matter of the Calf, *Ex.* 32. 4. with as little difguife as that of *Korah* and his Company. *David,* tho' a King, hath his adultery and murder difplay'd in the blackeft Characters : and King *Hezekiahs* little vanity of

I   fhewing

ſhewing his treaſures, do's not eſcape a remark.
Nay, even the reputation of their Nation
could not biaſs the Sacred Writers ; but they
freely tax their crimes : the Iſraelites murmu-
rings in the wilderneſs, their Idolatries in
Canaan, are ſet down without any palliation
or excuſe. And they are as frequently brand-
ed for their ſtubborneſs and ingratitude, as
the Canaanites are for their abominations.
So that certainly no Hiſtory in the world do's
better atteſt its truth by this evidence of impartiality.

5. In the laſt place it commends it ſelf
both by the pleaſure and profit it yields.
The rarity of thoſe events it records, ſurpriz-
es the mind with a delightful admiration;
and that mixture of ſage Diſcourſes, and
wellcoucht Parables wherewith it abounds,
do's at once pleaſe and inſtruct. How inge-
nouſly apt was *Nathans* Apologue to *David*,
whereby with Holy artifice he enſnar'd him into repentance ? And it remains ſtill matter of
inſtruction to us, to ſhew us with what unequal ſcales we are apt to weigh the ſame crime
in others and our ſelves. So alſo that long
train of ſmart calamities which ſucceeded his
ſin, is ſet out with ſuch particularity, that it
ſeems to be exactly the crime reverſt. His
own luſt with *Bathſheba*, was anſwer'd with
Amnons towards *Thamar* ; his murder of *Uriah*
with that of *Amnon* ; his treacherous contri-
yance

vance of that murder, with *Absoloms* traiterous conspiracy against him. So that every circumstance of his punishment, was the very Echo and reverberation of his guilt. A multitude of the like instances might be produc'd out of Holy Writ; all concurring to admonish us, that God exactly marks, and will repay our crimes; and that commonly with such propriety, that we need no other clue to guide us to the cause of our sufferings, than the very sufferings themselves. Indeed innumerable are the profitable observations arising from the Historical part of Scripture, that flow so easily and unconstrain'd, that nothing but a stupid inadvertence in the reader can make him baulk them: therefore 'twould be impertinent here to multiply instances.

6. LET us next consider the Prophetic part of Scripture, and we shall find it no less excellent in its kind. The Prophetick Books are for the most part made up (as the Prophetick Office was) of two parts; prediction and instruction. When God rais'd up Prophets, 'twas not only to acquaint men with future events, but to reform their present manners: and thefore as they are called Seers in one respect, so they are Watch-men and Shepherds in another. Nay, indeed the former was often subservient to the other as to the nobler end; their gift of fore-telling was to gain them authority, to be as it were the seal

of

of their commiffion ; to convince men that they were fent from God : and fo to render them the more pliant to their reproofs and admonitions. And the very matter of their prophecies was ufually adapted to this end : the denouncing of judgments being the moft frequent Theme, and that defign'd to bring men to repentance ; as appears experimentally in the cafe of *Nineveh.* And in this latter part of their office, the Prophets acted with the greateft incitation and vehemence.

7. W i t h what liberty and zeal do's *Elijah* arraign *Ahab* of *Naboths* murder, and foretell the fatal event of it, without any fear of his power, or reverence of his greatnefs? And *Samuel,* when he delivers *Saul* the fatal meffage of his rejection, do's paffionately and convincingly expoftulate with him concerning his fin, 1 *Sam.* 15. 17. Now the very fame Spirit ftill breaths in all the prophetick Writings : the fame truth of prediction, and the fame zeal againft vice.

8. F i r s t for the predictions, what fignal completions do we find ? How exactly are all the denunciations of judgments fulfill'd, where repentance has not interven'd ? He that reads the 28. chap. of *Deut.* and compares it with the Jews calamities, both under the Affyrians and Babylonians, and efpecially under the Romans, would think their oppreffors

preſſors had conſulted it, and tranſcrib'd their ſeverities thence. And even theſe Nations, who were the inſtruments of accompliſhing thoſe diſmal preſages, had their own ruins foretold, and as punctually executed. And as in Kingdoms and Nations, ſo to private perſons none of the prophetick threatnings ever return'd emty. The ſentence pronounc'd againſt *Ahab*, *Jezebel*, and their poſterity, was fulfill'd even to the moſt minute circumſtances of place and manner; as is evident by comparing the denunciation of *Elijah*, 1 Kings 21. 19. 23. with their tragical ends recorded in the following chapters. And as for *Jehu*, whoſe ſervice God was pleaſed to uſe in that execution, tho he rewarded it with entailing the crown of *Iſrael* on him for four deſcents; yet he fore-told thoſe ſhould be the limits: and accordingly we find *Zachariah*, the fourth deſcendent of his line, was the laſt of it that ſate on that throne, 2 *Kings* 15. 10. So alſo the deſtruction of *Achitophel* and *Judas*, the one immediate, the other many hundred years remote, are foretold by *David*, Pſal. 109. and we find exactly anſwer'd in the event.

9. NOR was this exactneſs confin'd only to the ſevere predictions, but as eminent in the more gracious. All the bleſſings which God by himſelf, or the Miniſtry of his Prophets promis'd, were ſtill infallibly made good.

At

At the time of life God return'd and visited *Sarah* with conception, notwithstanding those natural improbabilities which made her not only distrust, but even deride and laugh at the promise, *Gen.* 18. The posterity of that Son of Promise, the whole race of *Abraham* was deliver'd from the Egyptian bondage, and possest of *Canaan*, at the precise time which God had long before signified to *Abraham*, Gen. 15. So likewise the return of the Jews from the Babylonish captivity, was fore-told many years before their deportation, and *Cyrus* named for their restorer, before he had either name or being save only in Gods prescience, *If.* 44. 28. But I need not multiply instances of national or personal promises, The earliest, and most comprehensive promise of all was that of the Messiah, in whom all persons and *Nations of the world were to be blest*, Gen. 22. 11. *that seed of the woman that should bruise the Serpents head*, Gen. 3. 15. *To him give all the Prophets witness*, as Saint *Peter* observes, *Acts* 10. And he who was the subject, made himself also the expounder of those prophecies in his walk to *Emmaus* with the two Disciples, *Luk.* 24. 13. *beginning at* Moses, *and all the Prophets, he expounded to them in all the Scriptures, the things concerning himself.*

10. THIS as it was infinitly the greatest blessing afforded mankind, so was it the most
fre-

frequently and eminently predicted; and that with the moſt exact particularity as to all the circumſtances. His immaculate conception, the union of his two natures implied in his name *Immanuel*; *Behold a virgin ſhall conceive and bear a ſon, and ſhall call his name Immanuel*; is moſt plainly fore-told by *Iſ.* chap. 7. 14. Nay, the very place of his birth ſo punctually fore-told, that the Prieſts and Scribes could readily reſolve *Herods* queſtion upon the ſtrength of the Prophecy, and aſſure him Chriſt muſt be *born in Bethlehem*, Mat. 2. 5. As for the whole buſineſs and deſign of his life, we find it ſo deſcrib'd by *Iſaiah*, chap. 61. as Chriſt himſelf owns it, Luk. 4. 18. *The ſpirit of the Lord is upon me, becauſe he hath appointed me to preach good tidings to the meek; he hath ſent me to bind up the broken hearted, to proclaim liberty to the captives, and recovering of ſight to the blind, to ſet at liberty them that are bruiſed, to preach the acceptable year of the Lord.*

11. If we look farther to his death, the greateſt part of the Old Teſtament has a direct aſpect on it. All the Levitical œconomy of Sacrifices and Ablutions were but prophetick Rites, and ocular Predictions of that one expiatory Oblation. Nay, moſt of Gods providential diſpenſations to the Jews, carried in them types and prefigurations of this. Their reſcue from *Egypt*, the ſprin-
kling

kling of blood to fecure them from the de-
ftroying Angel; the Manna with which they
were fed, the Rock which fupplied them
water: thefe and many more referr'd to
Chrift, as their final and higheft fignifica-
tion.

12. B U T befides thefe darker adumbra-
tions, we have (as the Apoftle fpeaks) *a more
fure word of prophecy.* Saint *Peter* in his calcu-
lation begins with *Mofes,* takes in *Samuel,* and
the whole fucceffion of Prophets after him,
as bearing witnefs to this great event of
Chrifts paffion, *Acts* 4. 22. 24. And indeed he
that reads the Prophets confideringly, fhall
find it fo punctually defcrib'd, that the Evangelifts do not much more fully inftruct him
in the circumftances of it. *Daniel* tells us his
death, as to the kind of it, was to be violent:
The Meffiah fhall be cut off; and as to the defign of it 'twas *not for himfelf,* Dan. 9. 26. But
the Prophet *Ifaiah* gives us more than a bare
negative account of it; and exprefly faies,
*he was wounded for our tranfgreffions, he was
bruifed for our iniquities; the chaftifement of
our peace was on him, and by his ftripes we were
healed,* chap. 53. 5. And again, ver. 10. *Thou
fhalt make his Soul an offering for fin*; and ver.
11. *my righteous Servant fhall juftify many, for
he fhall bear their iniquities.* Nor is, *Job* an I-
dumean, much fhort of even this Evangelical
Prophet, in that fhort Creed of his, wherein he
owns

owns him as his Redeemer, *I know that my Redeemer liveth, &c.* Job. 19. 25.

13. AND as the end, so the circumstances of his sufferings are most of them under prediction : His extention upon the Cross is mention'd by the Psalmist : *They pierced my hands, and my feet ; I may tell all my bones,* Psal. 22. 16, 17. As for his inward dolours, they are in that Psalm so phathetically describ'd, that Christ chose that very form to breath them out in : *My God, my God, why hast thou forsaken me ?* ver. 1. So his revilers did also transcribe part of their reproaches from vers. 8. *He trusted in God ; let him deliver him now if he will have him,* Mat. 27. 43. That Vinegar which was offered him on the Cross, was a completion of a Prophecy ; *In my thirst they gave me Vinegar to drink,* Ps. 69. 21. the piercing of his side was expresly fore-told by *Zachary* ; *they shall look on him whom they have pierced,* Zach. 10. 12. The company in which he suffer'd, and the interment he had, are also intimated by *Isaiah, He made his Grave with the wicked, and with the rich in his death,* Isai. 53. 9. Nay even the disposal of his Garments was not without a Prophecy : *they parted my Garments among them, and upon my Vesture did they cast Lots,* Psal. 22. 18. Here are a cloud of witnesses which as they serve eminently to attest the truth of Christian Religion ; so do they to evince the excellency of Sacred Scrip-

K   ture ;

ture ; as to the verity of the Prophetick part.

14. As to the admonitory part of the Prophetick Writings, they are in their kind no way inferior to the other. The reproofs are autoritative and convincing. What piercing exprobrations do we find of *Israels* ingratitude ? How often are they upbraided with the better examples of the bruit Creatures ? with the Ox and the Ass by *Isaiah*, Chap. 1. 3. with the Stork, and the Crane, and the Swallow, by *Jeremiah*, Chap. 8. 7. Nay the constancy of the Heathen to their false Gods is instanc'd to reproach their revolt from the true. *Hath a Nation chang'd their Gods which yet are no Gods ? but my People have chang'd their Glory for that which doth not profit,* Jer. 2. 11. What awful, what Majestick representations do we find of Gods power, to awake their dread ! *Fear ye not me saith the Lord ? will ye not tremble at my presence ; who have plac'd the Sands for the bounds of the Sea by a perpetual decree, that it cannot pass over ; and tho' the Waves thereof toss themselves, yet can they not prevail; tho' they roar, yet can they not pass over it,* Jer. 22. And again, *Thus saith the High and lofty one that inhabiteth Eternity, whose name is Holy : I dwell in the High and Holy Place,* Is. 57. 15. So we find him describ'd as *a God Glorious in Holiness, fearful in Praises, doing Wonders,* Ex. 15. 11. These and many other the like heights of Divine eloquence we meet

meet with in the Prophetick Writings : which cannot but strike us with an awful reverence of the Divine Power.

15. N O R are they less Pathetick in the gentler strains. What instance is there of the greatest tenderness and love, which God has not adopted to express his by ? He personates all the nearest and most endearing relations : that of a Husband ; *I will Marry thee to my self,* Hos. 2. 19. of a Father ; *I am a Father to* Israel, *and* Ephraim *is my first Born* : nay, he vies Bowels with the tender Sex, and makes it more possible for a Mother to renounce her *compassions towards the Son of her Womb,* than for him to with-draw his, *Isa.* 49. 15. By all these endearments, these *cords of a man,* these *bands of love,* as himself stiles them, *Hos.* 11. 4. endeavouring to draw his people to their duty, and their happiness. And when their perverseness frustrates all this his Holy Artifice ; how passionately do's he expostulate with them ? how solemnly protest his averseness to their ruin ? *Why will ye die O House of* Israel ? *for I have no pleasure in the death of him that dieth, saith the Lord God,* Ezek. 18. 31, 32. with what regrets and relenting do's he think of abandoning them ? *How shall I give thee up* Ephraim ? *How shall I deliver thee* Israel ? *How shall I make thee as* Admah ! *How shall I set thee as* Zeboim ? *my Heart is turn'd within me, my repentings are kindled together* ; Hos.

11. 8. In ſhort, 'twere endleſs to cite the places in theſe Prophetick Books, wherein God do's thus condeſcend to ſolicit even the ſenſitive part of man ; and that with ſuch moving Rhetorick, that I cannot but wonder at the exception ſome of our late Cricks make againſt the Bible, for its defect in that particular ; for Oratory is nothing but a dextrous application to the affections and paſſions of men. And certainly we find not that done with greater advantage any where than in Sacred Writ.

16. Yᴇᴛ it was not the deſign of the Prophets (no more than of the Apoſtle) to take men with guile ; 2 *Cor.* 12. 16. to inveigle their affections unawares to their underſtandings ; but they addreſs as well to their reaſons, make ſolemn appeals to their judicative faculties. And *now judge I pray between me and my Vinyard*, ſays *Iſa.* 5. 3. Nay, God by the Prophet *Ezekiel* ſolemnly pleads his own cauſe before them, vindicates the equity of his proceedings from the aſperſions they had caſt on them ; and by moſt irrefragable Arguments refutes that injurious Proverb which went currant among them ; and in the cloſe appeals to themſelves, *O Houſe of* Iſrael *are not my ways equal? are not your ways unequal?* Ezek. 18. the evidences were ſo clear that he remits the matter to their own determination. And generally we ſhall find that among
all

all the Topicks of difwafion from fin, there is none more clofely preft, than that of the folly of it. Idolatry was a fin to which *Ifrael* had a great propenfion, and againft which moft of the Prophets admonitions were directed. And certainly it can never be more expos'd, and the fottifh unreafonablenefs of it better difplay'd, than we find it in the 44. Chap. of *Ifaiah.* In like manner we may read the Prophet *Jeremy* difwading from the fame fin by Arguments of the moft irrefragable conviction, *Jer.* 10.

17. AND as the Prophets omitted nothing as to the manner of their addrefs, to render their exhortations effectual, the matter of them was likewife fo confiderable as to command attention; It was commonly either the recalling them from their revolts and Apoftacies from God by Idolatry, or elfe to convince them of the infignificancy of all thofe legal Ceremonial performances they fo much confided in, when taken up as a *fuperfedeas* to moral duties. Upon this account it is, that they often depreciate, and in a manner prohibit the folemneft of their Worfhips. *To what purpofe are the multitude of your Sacrifices unto me ? bring no more vain Oblations: incenfe is an abomination to me ; the new Moons and fabbaths, the calling of Affemblies I cannot away with : it is Iniquity even your folemn meetings,* &c. If. 1. 11. 13. Not that thefe

things

things were in themselves reprovable; for they were all commanded by God; but because the Jews depended so much on these external observances, that they thought by them to commute for the *weightier matters of the Law* (as our Saviour after stiles them) *Judgment, Mercy and Faith,* Mat. 23. 23. lookt on these rites which discriminated them from other Nations, as dispensations from the universal obligations of nature and common justice.

18. THIS deceit of theirs is sharply ubbraided to them by the Prophet *Jeremy;* where he calls their boasts of the *Temple of the Lord, the Temple of the Lord, lying words;* and on the contrary, lays the whole stress of their obedience, and expectation of their happiness on the justice and innocence of their conversation, Ch. 7. 4. And after do's smartly reproach their insolence in boldly resorting to that house, which by bringing their sins along with them, they made but an Asylum, and Sanctuary for those crimes. *Will ye steal, murder and commit adultery, and swear falsely, and burn incense to* Baal, *and walk after other Gods whom ye know not, and come and stand before me in this house? Is this house which is called by my name become a Den of robbers in your eyes?* Chap. 7. 9, 10, 11. Indeed all the Prophets seem to conspire in this one design, of making them look thro' shadows and ceremonies,

nies, to that inward purity, Justice and Honesty, which they were design'd to inculcate, not to supplant.   And this design as it is in it self most excellent, most worthy the command of God, and the nature of man; so we have seen that it has bin pursued by all the most apt, and most powerful mediums, that the thing or persons addrest to were capable of; and so that the Prophets are no less eminent for the discharge of this exhortatory part of their office, than they were in the former, of the predicting.

19. The next part of Scripture we are to consider, is the Doctrinal; by which I shall not in this place understand the whole complex of Faith and Manners together; but restrain it only to those Revelations which are the object of our Belief; and these are so sublime, as shews flesh and blood never reveal'd them.   Those great mysteries of our Faith, the Trinity, the Incarnation, the Hypostatical union, the Redemption of the world by making the offended party the Sacrifice for the offence; are things of so high and abstruse speculation, as no finite understanding can fully fathom.   I know their being so, is by some made an Argument for disbelief; but doubtless, very injustly : for (not to insist upon the different natures of Faith and Science, by which that becomes a proper object of the one which is not of the other) our
non-

non-comprehenſion is rather an indication that they have a higher riſe ; and renders it infinitely improbable that they could ſpring from mans invention. For 'twere to ſuppoſe too great a diſproportion between human faculties to think men could invent what themſelves could not underſtand. Indeed theſe things ly ſo much out of the road of human imagination, that I dare appeal to the breſts of the moſt perverſe gain-ſayers, whether ever they could have fallen into their thoughts without ſuggeſtion from without. And therefore 'tis a malicious contradiction to reject theſe truths becauſe of their diſſonancy from human reaſon, and yet at the ſame time to aſcribe their original to man. But certainly there can be nothing more inconſiſtent with mere natural reaſon, than to think God can be or do no more than man can comprehend. Never any Nation or perſon that own'd a Deity, did ever attempt ſo to circumſcribe him : and it is proportionable only to the licentious profaneſs of theſe latter days, thus to meaſure immenſity and omnipotence by our narrow ſcantling.

20. T H E more genuine and proper effect of theſe ſupernatural truths is, to raiſe our admiration of that divine Wiſdom, *whoſe ways are ſo paſt finding out* ; and to give us a juſt ſenſe of that infinite diſtance which is between it, and the higheſt of that reaſon wherein we

ſo

so pride our selves. And the great propriety these Doctrines have to that end, may well be reckon'd as one part of their excellency.

21. INDEED there is no part of our holy Faith, but is naturally productive of some peculiar virtue ; as the whole Scheme together engages us to be universally *Holy in all manner of conversation.* 1 Pet. 1. 15. And it is the supereminent advantage true Religion hath over all false ones, that it tends to so laudable an end.

22. THE Theology of the Heathens was in many instances an extract and quintessence of vice. Their most solemn Rites, and Sacred'st Mysteries were of such a nature, that instead of refining and elevating, they corrupted and debased their Votaries ; immerst them in all those abominable pollutions which sober nature abhorr'd. Whereas the principles of our Faith serve to spiritualize and rectifie us, to raise us as much above mere manhood as theirs cast them below it.

23. AND as they are of this vast advantage to us, so also are they just to God, in giving us right notions of him. What vile unworthy apprehensions had the Heathen of their Deities ; intitling them not only to the passions but even to the crimes of men : making *Jupiter* an adulterer, *Mercury* a thief, *Bacchus* a drunkard , *&c.* proportionably of the rest ? Whereas our God is represented to us as an

L essence,

effence, fo fpiritual, and incorporeal, that we muſt be unbodied our felves before we can perfectly conceive what he is : fo far from the impotent affections and inclinations of men, that he has neither parts, nor paſſions ; and is fain to veil himſelf under that difguife, to fpeak fometimes as if he had, merely in con-defcention to our groffer faculties.　And a-gain, fo far from being an example, a patron of vice, that his *eyes are too pure to behold iniquity*, Hab. 1. 13.　Holineſs is an effential part of his nature, and he muſt denie himſelf to put it off.

24. THE greateſt defcent that ever he made to humanity, was in the incarnation of the fecond perfon : yet even in that, tho' he was linked with a finful nature, yet he preferv'd the perfon immaculate ; and while he had all the fins of the world upon him by imputation, fuffer'd not any one to be inherent in him.

25. To conclude, the Scripture deſcribes our God to us by all thofe glorious Attributes of infinity, Power and Juſtice, which may ren-der him the proper object of onr Adorations and Reverence : and it difcribes him alfo in thofe gentler Attributes of Goodneſs, Mer-cy and Truth, which may excite our love of, and dependance on him.　Thefe are reprefen-tations fomething worthy of God, and fuch as impreſs upon our mind great thoughts of him.

26. BUT

26. BUT never did the Divine Attributes so concur to exert themselves, as in the mystery of our Redemption: where his Justice was satisfied without diminution to his Mercy ; and his Mercy without entrenching on his Justice : his Holiness most eminent in his indignation against sin, and yet his Love no less so in sparing sinners : these contradictions being reconcil'd, this discord compos'd into harmony by his infinite Wisdom. This is that stupendous Mystery into which *the Angels desir'd to look,* 1 Pet. 1. 12. And this is it which by *the Gospel is preach'd unto us* ; as it follows, ver. 25.

27. AND as the Scripture gives us this knowledge of God, so it do's also of our selves ; in which two, all profitable knowledge is comprised. It teaches us how vile we were in our original dust ; and how much viler yet in our fall, which would have sunk us below our first principles, sent us not only to earth, but hell. It shews the impotence of our lapsed estate ; that we are not *able of our selves so much as to think a good thought* : and it shews us also the dignity of our renovated estate, that we *are heirs of God, and fellow-heirs with Christ,* Rom. 8. 17. yet lest this might puff us up with mistaken hopes ; it plainly acquaints us with the condition on which this depends ; that it must be our obedience both active and passive, which is to intitle us to it : that we

L 2 must

muſt *be faithful to death, if we mean to inherit a crown of Life,* Rev. 2. 10. and that *we muſt ſuffer with Chriſt, if we will be glorified with him,* Rom. 8. 17.   And upon ſuppoſition that we perform our parts of the condition, it gives us the moſt certain aſſurance, engages Gods veracity that he will not fail on his.   By this it gives us ſupport againſt all the adverſities of life ; aſſuring us *the ſufferings of it are not worthy to be compared with the glory we exſpect,* Rom. 8. 18. yea, and againſt the terrors of death too ; by aſſuring us that what we look on as a diſſolution, is but a temporary parting ; and we only put off our bodies, that they may put off corruption, and be cloathed with immortality.

28. THESE and the like are the Doctrines the Holy Scripture offers to us : and we may certainly ſay, they are *faithful ſayings,* and *worthy of all acceptation,* 1 Tim. 4. 9.   The notions it gives us of God are ſo ſublime and great, that they cannot but affect us with reverence, and admiration : and yet withall, ſo amiable and endearing that they cannot but raiſe love and gratitude, affiance and delight. ——

29. AND, which is yet more, the milder Attributes are apt to inſpirit us with a generous ambition of aſſimilation ; excite us to tranſcribe all his imitable excellencies : in which the very Heathens could diſcern conſiſted

fifted the accomplishment of human felicity.

30. A N D then the knowledge it gives us of our selves, do's us the kindest office imaginable : keeps us from those swelling thoughts we are too apt to entertain, and shews us the necessity of bottoming our hopes upon a firmer foundation : and then again keeps us from being lazy or secure, by shewing us the necessity of our own endeavours. In a word, it teaches us to be humble and industrious, and whoever is so ballasted can hardly be shipwrackt.

31. T H E S E are the excellencies of the Doctrinal part of the Scriptures, which also renders them most aptly preparative for the preceptive. And indeed, so they were design'd : the *Credenda* and the *Agenda* being such inseparable relations, that whoever parts them, forfeits the advantage of both. The most solemn profession of Christ, the most importunate invocations, Lord, Lord, will signifie nothing to them *which do not the things which he says.* Mat. 7. And how excellent, how rational those precepts are which the Scripture proposes to us from him, is our next point of consideration.

32. T H E first Law which God gave to mankind was that of nature. And tho' the impressions of it upon the mind be by *Adams* fall exceedingly dimm'd and defac'd ; yet
that

that derogates nothing from the dignity and worth of that Law, which God has bin so far from cancelling, that he seems to have made it the rule and square of his subsequent Laws: so that nothing is injoin'd in those, but what is consonant and agreeable to that. The Moral Law given in the Decalogue to the Jews, the Evangelical Law given in the Gospel to Christians, have this natural Law for their basis and foundation. They licence nothing which that prohibits, and very rarely prohibit any thing which it licences.

33. 'Tis true, Christ in his Sermon on the Mount, raises Christians to a greater strictness than the Jews thought themselves oblig'd to; but that was not by contradicting either the natural, or moral Law, but by rescuing the later from those corruptions which the false glosses of the Scribes and Pharisees had mixt with it; and reducing it to its primitive integrity, and extent. In a word, as the Decalogue was given to repair the Defacings, and renew the impressions of the natural Law; so the precepts of the Gospel were design'd to revive and illustrate both. And accordingly we find Christ, in the matter of Divorce, calls them back to this natural Law; *In the begining it was not so*, Mat. 19. 8. I say not but that even these natural notions are in some instances refin'd and elevated by Christ; the second *Adam* being to repair the fall of the first

with

with advantage : but yet he ftill builds upon that ground-work, introduces nothing that is inconfiftent with it.

34. A N D this accordance between thefe feveral Laws is a circumftance that highly recommends Scripture precepts to us. We cannot imagine but that God who made man for no other end but to be an inftrument of his glory ; and a recipient of all communicable parts of his happinefs, would affign him fuch rules and meafures as were moft conducive to thofe ends. And therefore fince the Scripture injunctions are of the fame mould, we muft conclude them to be fuch as tend to the perfection of our being ; the making us what God originally intended us : and he that would not be that, will certainly chufe much worfe for himfelf,

35. I know there have bin prejudices taken up againft the precepts of Chrift, as if they impos'd unreafonable, unfupportable ftrictneffes upon men : and fome have affum'd liberty to argue mutinoufly againft them ; nay, againft God too for putting fuch natural appetites into men, and then forbidding them to fatisfie them.

36. B U T the ground of this cavil is the not rightly diftinguifhing of natural appetites, which are to be differenc'd according to the two ftates of rectitude and depravation : thofe of the firft rank are the appetites

God

God put into man ; and thoſe were all regular and innocent, ſuch as tended to the preſervation of his being : nature in its firſt integrity meaſuring its deſires by its needs.   Now
Chriſts prohibitions are not directed againſt
theſe, he forbids no one kind of theſe deſires.
And tho' the precept of ſelf-denial may ſometimes reſtrain us in ſome particular acts; yet
that is but proportionable to that reſtraint
Adam was under in relation to the forbidden
tree, a particular inſtance of his obedience,
and fence of his ſafety.   So that if men would
conſider nature under this its firſt and beſt notion, they cannot accuſe Chriſt of being ſevere to it.

37. B U T 'tis manifeſt they take it in another acception, and mean that corruption of
nature which inordinately inclines to ſenſitive
things ; and on this account they call their
riots, their luxuries, appetites put into them
by God : whereas 'tis manifeſt this was ſuper-
induced from another coaſt : The wiſe man
gives us its true pedigree in what he ſays of
death, which is its twin-ſiſter : *By the envy of
the devil came death into the world,* Wiſ. 2. 24.
And can they expect that Chriſt who came to
deſtroy the works of the devil, 1 Joh. 3. 8. ſhould
frame Laws in their favour, make Acts of to-
leration and indulgence for them ? This were
to annul the whole deſign of his coming into
the world, which was to reſtore us from our
                                            lapſt

lapft eftate, and elevate us to thofe higher degrees of purity which he came not only to prefcribe, but to exemplifie to us.

38. BUT in this affair men often take nature in a yet wider and worfe notion; and under natural defires comprehend whatever upon any fort of motive they have a mind to do. The aw of a fuperior, the importunity of a companion, cuftom, and example, make men do many ill things, to which their nature would never promt them; nay, many times fuch as their nature relucts to, and abhors. 'Tis certainly thus in all debauchery and excefs. 'Tis evident, it gratifies no mans nature to be drunk, or to lie under undigefted loads of meats: thefe are out-rages and violences upon nature, take it only in the moft fenfitive notion, fuch as fhe ftruggles to avert: and yet men make her bear, not only the oppreffion, but the blame too.

39. BUT befides 'tis to be confider'd, that the nature of a man includes reafon as well as fenfe, and to this all forts of luxury are yet more repugnant, as that which clouds the mind, and degrades the man (who in his conftitution is a rational being) and fets him in the rank of mere animals: and certainly thefe can be no appetites of nature, which thus fubvert it.

40. THE like may be faid concerning revenge, particularly that abfurdeft fort of it,

M   duels,

duels; which certainly are as great contradictions to nature as can be imagin'd, the unra-
velling and cancelling its very firſt principle
of ſelf-preſervation, (which in other inſtan-
ces men bring in bar againſt duty.) And yet
men will ſay the generoſity of their natures
compels them to it ; ſo making their natures a kind of *felo de ſe* to promt the de-
ſtroying it ſelf: when alas 'tis only the falſe
notion they have got of honour that ſo engages them.   And if men would but ſoberly
conſider, they muſt be convinc'd that there
is nothing more agreeable to reaſon than
that precept of Chriſt of not retaliating injuries ; which is in effect but to bid us to chuſe
a ſingle inconvenience before a long train of
miſchiefs.   And certainly if nature even in
its deprav'd eſtate were left to determine, it
would reſolve it a better bargain to go off
with a reproachful word, than to loſe a limb,
perhaps a life in the revenge of it.   There
being no maxim more indiſputable, than
that of evils the leaſt is to be choſen.   And
the innate principle of ſelf-love do's more
ſtrongly biaſs nature to preſerve it ſelf, than
any external thing can to deſtroy it.

41. I know 'twill be ſaid to this, that revenge is a natural appetite : but I ſay ſtill, ſelf-
preſervation is more ſo ; and would prevail
againſt as much of revenge as is natural, were
it not heightned and fortified by phancy, and
                                                       that

that Chimera of point of honour, which, as it is now stated, is certainly one of the most empty nothings that ever was brought in balance with solid interests.   And indeed 'tis to belie nature, and suppose it to have forfeited all degrees of reason, as well as vertue, to fasten so absurd a choice upon her.   But admit revenge to be never so much the dictate of corrupt nature; 'tis certain 'tis not of primitive regular nature.   Revenge is but a relative to injury : and he that will say God put the appetite of revenge into man, must say he put the appetite of injury into him also : which is such an account of the sixth days creation, as is hardly consistent with Gods own testimony of its being *very good*, Gen. 1.

42. Besides, 'tis certain all the desires God infus'd into human nature, were such as tended to its preservation ; but this of revenge, is of all other the most destructive as is too sadly attested by the daily tragical effects of it.   In short, the wise-man gives us a good summary of the whole matter: *God made man upright, but he sought out many inventions,* Eccl. 7. 29.

43. Now if man have by his own voluntary act deprav'd himself, it would be neither just nor kind in God to warp his Laws to mans now distorted frame; but it is both, to keep up the perfect rectitude of those, and call upon man to reduce himself to a con-

formity with them : and when to this is added
fuch a fupply of grace as may filence the plea
of difability, there can nothing be imagin'd
more worthy of God, or more indulgent to
man.

44. A ND all this Chrift do's in the Gofpel,
in thofe precepts which the blind world
makes the fubject of their cavil or fcorn.
It were an eafie task to evince this in every
particular precept of the Gofpel; but I fhall
content my felf with the inftances already
given, and not fwell this Tract by infifting
upon what has already bin the fubject of fo
many pious and excellent difcourfes, as muft
already have convinc'd all but the obftinate.

45. W E proceed therefore to a view of
the promiffory parts of Scripture; in which
we are firft in general to obferve the great
goodnefs of God, in making any promifes
at all to us; and next to examine of what nature and excellence thefe promifes are. And
firft if we confider how many titles God has
to our obedience, we muft acknowledge he
may challenge it as his undoubted right.
We are the work of his hands ; and if the
Potter have power over the clay (the mate-
rials whereof are not of his making) much
more has God over his creatures, whofe matter as well as form is wholly owing to him.
We are the price of his blood. And if men
account purchafe an indefeifible title, God
must

muſt have abſolute dominion over what he has bought, and at ſo dear a price too as his own blood. Laſtly we depend upon him for the ſupport of that being he has given us : we live merely upon his bounty, ſpend upon his ſtock. And what Patron will not expect obſervance from one who thus ſubſiſts by him ?

46. YET as if God had none of theſe claims, theſe preingagements upon us, he deſcends to treat with us as free-men, by way of Article and compact ; buy's his own of us, and engages to reward that obedience, which he might upon the utmoſt penalties exact : which is ſuch an aſtoniſhing indulgence as our higheſt gratitude cannot reach : and of this the Sacred Scriptures are the evidences and records ; and therefore upon that account deſerve at once our reverence, and our joy.

47. BUT this will yet farther appear, if we look in the ſecond place into the promiſes themſelves ; which are ſo extenſive as to take in both our preſent and future ſtate : according to that of the Apoſtle ; *Godlineſs hath the promiſe of this Life, and of that which is to come,* 1 Tim, 4. 8. For the preſent, they are proportion'd to the ſeveral parts of our compoſition ; the body, and the mind, the outward and the inward man ; ſo ſtretching themſelves to all we can really be concern'd for in this world.

48. AND firſt for the body, the Old Teſtament

ſtament abounds in promiſes of this ſort. The firſt part of the 28. of _Deut._ contains a full catalogue of all temporal bleſſings ; and thoſe irreverſibly entail'd upon the Iſraelites obedience , ver. 1. The Pſalmiſt tells us, _they that fear the Lord ſhall lack nothing,_ Pſ. 34. 9. _that they ſhall not be confounded in the perillous time, and in the days of dearth they ſhall have enough,_ Pſ. 37. 19. And _Solomon, that the Lord will not ſuffer the righteous to famiſh,_ Pro. 10. 3. And tho' under the Goſpel, the promiſes of temporal affluence ſeem not ſo large; (its deſign being to ſpiritualize us, and raiſe our minds to higher injoyments;) yet it gives us ample ſecurity of ſo much as is really good for us. It ſuperſedes our care for our ſelves by aſſuring us _all theſe things ſhall be added to us,_ Mat. 6. 33. that is, _all thoſe things which our heavenly Father knows we have need of,_ ver. 32. which is all the limitation the context gives. And certainly we have little temptation to fear want, who have him for our provider; _whoſe are all the beaſts of the Forreſt, and the cattel upon a thouſand hills,_ Pſ. 50. 10.

49. And when we are thus ſecur'd of all things neceſſary, it may perhaps be an equal mercy to ſecure us from great abundance; which at the beſt, is but a _lading ones ſelf with thick clay,_ in the Prophets phraſe, _Hab._ 2. 6. but is often a ſnare as well as a burden.

50. Besides, the Goſpel by its precepts
of

of temperance and self-denial, do's so con-
tract our appetites, that a competence is a
more adequate promise to them, than that of
superfluity would have bin; and 'tis also the
measure wherein all the true satisfaction of
the senses consists; which are gratified with
moderate pleasures, but suffocated and over-
whelm'd with excessive. The temperate man
tastes and relishes his portion, whilst the voluptuous may rather be said to wallow in his
plenty than injoy it.

51. AND as the necessaries of life, so life
it self, and the continuance of that, is a Scripture promise. The fifth Commandment af-
fixes it to one particular duty : but it is in a
multitude of places in the Old Testament an-
nex'd to general obedience. Thus it is, *Deut.*
11. 9. and again, ver. 21. And *Solomon* proposes this practical wisdom as the multiplier
of days : *By me thy days shall be multiplied,
and the years of thy life shall be increas'd,* Pro.
9. 11. and chap. 3. *Length of days is in her
right hand,* ver. 16. And tho' we find not
this promise repeated in the New Testament,
yet neither is it retracted : 'tis true, the Gospel bids us be ready to lay down our lives
for Christs sake, but it tells us withal, that he
that will lose his life, shall save it : which tho'
it be universally true only in the spiritual
sense, yet it often proves so in a literal. It
did so eminently in the destruction of *Jerusalem,*

lem, where the most resolute Christians e-
scap'd, while the base compliers perish'd together with those they sought to endear. This
is certain, that if the New Testament do'not
expresly promise long life, yet it do's by its
rules of temperance and sobriety, contented-
ness and chearfulness, very much promote it:
and so do's virtually and efficaciously ratifie
those the Old Testament made.

52. THE next outward blessing is reputation : and this also is a Scripture promise. *The wise shall inherit glory,* Prov. 3. 35.
And the vertuous woman *Solomon* describes,
is not only blessed by her children and husband, but *she is prais'd in the gate,* Pro. 31. *ult.*
Nay, this blessing is extended even beyond
life : *The memory of the just shall be blessed,*
Prov. 10. 7. Nor do's the Gospel evacuate
this promise; but rather prompts us to the ways
of having it made good to us, by advising us
to *abstain from all appearance of evil,* 1. Thes. 5.
22. *to provide for honest things, not only in the
sight of God, but also in the sight of men,* 2. Cor.
8. 21.

53. 'T IS true indeed, Christ fore-warns
his Disciples that they shall be revil'd, and
*have all manner of evil spoken against them falsly,
for his names sake :* but then the cause trans-
form'd the sufferings, and made it so honour-
able, that they were *to count it matter of joy,*
Mat. 5. 11, 12. Neither was this any para-
dox

dox even in relation to their reputation; which tho' fullied by a few ill men of that age, yet has bin moſt illuſtrious among all Ages fince. Their ſufferings and indignities gave them a new title of honour, and added the Martyr to the Apoſtle. And the event has bin proportionable in all ſucceſſions fince: Thoſe Holy men that fill'd up the Pagan priſons, fill'd up the Churches Diptycks alſo, and have bin had as the Pſalmiſt ſpeaks, *in everlaſting remembrance,* Pſ. 112. 6.

54. AND as Scripture-promiſes thus take in all the concerns of the outward man, ſo do they alſo of the inward. The fundamental promiſe of this kind, is that of *ſending Chriſt into the world,* and *in him eſtabliſhing the new Covenant,* which we find, *Jer.* 31. 31. and is referr'd to by the Author to the Hebrews, *I will put my Laws in their hearts, and write them in their minds ; and their ſins and iniquities will I remember no more,* Heb. 10. 16.

55. AND this is ſo comprehenſive a promiſe as includes all the concerns of the inward man. The evils incident to the mind of man may be reduc'd to two; impurity, and inquietude : and here is a cure to both. The divine Law written in the heart, drives thence all thoſe ſwarms of noyſom luſts, which like the Egyptian Frogs over-run and putrifie the ſoul. Where that is ſeated and enſhrin'd, thoſe can no more ſtand before it, than *Da-*

gon

gon before the Ark. This repairs the divine Image in us (in which confifts the perfection of our nature) *renews us in the fpirits of our minds* , Eph. 4. 23. *and purges our confciences from dead works,* Heb. 9. 14. which all the Catharticks and Luftrations among the Heathen, all the facrifices and ceremonies of the Law were not able to do.

56. SECONDLY, this promife fecures the mind from that reftlefnefs and unquietnefs, which attends both the dominion and guilt of fin. To be fubject to a mans lufts and corrupt appetites is of all others the vileft vaffallage : they are the cruelleft task-mafters, and allow their flaves no reft, no intermiffion of their drudgery. And then again, the guilt that tortures and racks the mind with dreadful expectations, keeps it in perpetual agitation and tumult ; which is excellently defcrib'd by the Prophet *Ifaiah, The wicked is like the troubled fea, when it cannot reft ; whofe waters caft out mire and dirt : there is no peace faith my God to the wicked,* If. 48. 22. How profperous foever vice may feem to be in the world, yet there are fuch fecret pangs and horrors that dog it, that as *Solomon* fays, *even in laughter the heart is forrowful,* Prov. 14. 13.

57. BUT this Evangelical promife of being *merciful to our iniquities, and remembring our fins no more,* calms this tempeft, introduces peace and ferenity into the mind, and re-
conciles

conciles us at once to God and our selves. And sure we may well say with the Apostle, these are *great and precious promises,* 2 Pet. 1. 4.

58. There are besides many other which spring from these principles, as suckers from the root : such are the promises of fresh supplies of grace upon a good imployment of the former. *To him that hath shall be given,* Mat. 25. 29. Nay, even of the source and fountain of all grace. *He shall give the Holy spirit to them that ask him,* Mat. 7. 11. Such is that of supporting us in all difficulties and assaults : *the not suffering us to be tempted above that we are able,* 1. Cor. 10. 13. which like Gods *bow set in the clouds,* Gen. 9. is our security, that we shall not be over-whelm'd by any deluge of temptation : and (to instance no more) such is that comprehensive promise of hearing our prayers, *Ask and it shall be given you,* Mat. 7. 7. This puts all good things within our reach, gives us the key of Gods Storehouse, from whence we may furnish our selves with all that is really good for us. And if a few full Barns could tempt the rich man in the Gospel, to pronounce a Requiem to his soul; what notes of acquiescence may they sing, who have the command of an inexhaustible store ; that are supplied by him whose is the earth, and the fulness thereof?

59. And certainly, all the promises to-

gether muft be (to ufe the Apoftles phrafe)
ftrong confolation ; fuch as may quiet and calm
all the fears and griefs, all the tumults and
perturbations of the mind, in relation to its
prefent ftate.   But then there are others relating to the future of a much higher eleva-
tion : thofe glories and felicities of another
world, which are fo far beyond our narrow
conceptions, that the comprehenfion and in-
joyment muft begin together.   The Scripture
fhadows it out to us by all the notions we have
of happinefs : by *glory,* Rom. 8. 18. by a *kingdom,* Mat. 25. 14. by *joy,* Mat. 25. 21. and
which comprehends all, by *being with the Lord,*
1 Thef. 4. 17. *feeing him face to face,* 1 Cor.
13. 12. *being like to him,* 1 Jo. 3. 2.   In a word
'tis *blifs* in the utmoft extent : immenfe for
quantity, and eternal for duration.

60. A N D furely this promife is fo excellent
in its kind, fo liberal in its degree, fo tranfcendently great in all refpects, that did it ftand
fingle, ftript of all thofe that relate to this life,
it alone would juftifie the name of Gofpel, and
be the beft tidings that ever came to mankind.
For alas, if we compare the hopes that other
Religions propofe to their Votaries with thefe,
how bafe, how ignoble are they ! The Heathens Elyfium, the Mahumetan Paradife, were
but higher gratifications of the fenfual part,
and confequently were depreffions and debafe-
ments of the rational. So that in effect they
                                   provided

provided a heaven for the beast, and a hell for the man. We may therefore confidently refume our conclufion, and pronounce the Scripture promifes to be fo divine and excellent, that they could as little have bin made, as they can be perform'd by any but an Holy and Almighty Author.

61. NOR is their being conditional any impeachment to their worth, but an enhanfement. Should God have made them (as fome phancy he has his decrees) abfolute and irrefpective; he had fet his promifes at war with his precepts, and thefe fhould have fuperfeded what thofe injoyn. We are all very niggardly towards God, and fhould have bin apt to have ask'd *Judas's* queftion; *to what purpofe is this wafte?* Mat. 26. 8. What needs the labour of the courfe if the prize be certain? And it muft have bin infinitely below the wifdom and majefty of the fupreme Legiflator, to make Laws, and then evacuate them by difpencing rewards without any refpect to their obfervance. 'Tis the Sanction which infpirits the Law, without which the divine, as well as the human, would to moft men be a *dead letter*.

62. BUT againft this God has abundantly provided, not only by the conditionality of the promifes, but by the terrour of his threats too; which is the laft part of Scripture which falls under confideration. And thefe are of the

the moſt direful kinds; and cannot better be illuſtrated than by the oppoſition they ſtand in to the promiſes : for as thoſe included all things that might make men happy either as to this life or the next; ſo theſe do all that may make them miſerable. If we make our reflection on all the particulars of the promiſes, we ſhall find the threats anſwering them as their reverſe or dark ſhadow.

63. And firſt as concerning the outward ſtate, if we look but into the 28 of *Deut.* we ſhall find, that after all the gracious promiſes which begun the chapter, it finally ends in thunder, in the moſt dreadful denunciations imaginable ; and thoſe adapted by a moſt peculiar oppoſition to the former promiſes : as the Reader may ſee at large in that Chapter. And the whole tenour of the Sripture go's in the like ſtile. Thus, Pſal. 140. 11. *A wicked perſon ſhall not proſper in the earth, evil ſhall hunt the wicked man to overthrow him. The Lord will not ſuffer the righteous to famiſh, but he caſteth out the ſubſtance of the wicked*; Pro. 10. 3. And again, the *righteous eateth to the ſatisfying of his ſoul, but the belly of the wicked ſhall want*, Pro. 13. 25. Multitudes of like general threatnings of temporal improſperity there are every where ſcatter'd throughout the Scripture ; and many more applied to particular vices, as ſloth, unmercifulneſs, luxury, and the

the like ; which would be here too long to enumerate.

64. AND altho' thefe threatnings may feem fometimes to be litterally confuted by the wealth and opulency of wicked men, yet they never mifs of being really and vertually verified. For either their profperities are very fhort, and only preparative to a more eminent ruin, which was the Pfalmifts refolution of this doubt, *Pfal.* 73. or elfe if God leave them the matter of temporal happinefs, yet he fubftracts the vertue and fpirit of them, renders them empty and unfatisfying. This is well expreft by the Pfalmift in the cafe of the Ifraelites : *He gave them their defire, and fent leanefs withall into their foul,* Pf. 106. 15, and by *Zophar,* Job 20. 22. where fpeaking of the wicked, he faith ; *In the fulnefs of his fufficiency fhall he be in ftraits.* And to this *Solomon* feems to refer, when he faith, *the bleffing of the Lord maketh rich, and he addeth no forrow with it,* Pro. 10. 22.

65. NEITHER is it only the comforts of life, but life it felf that is threatned to be taken from wicked men : untimely death is thro'-out the Old Teftament frequently mention'd as the guerdon of impiety : 'tis often affign'd judicially in particular cafes : *He fhall be cut off from his people,* being the ufual fentence upon moft offenders under the Levitical Law. But 'tis alfo menaced more generally as an

imme-

immediate judgment from God : *The blood-thirsty and deceitful men shall not live out half their days*, Psal. 55. 23.   Farther yet, their names shall putrifie as soon as their Carkasses : *the name of the wicked shall rot* ; Pro. 10. 7.   Nay both their infamy and their ruin are intail'd upon their posterity. *The seed of the evil doers shall never be renown'd. Prepare slaughter for his children, for the iniquity of their fathers* ; Isa. 14. 20, 21.

66. I F now we look on Scripture threat-nings in relation to the mind of man, we shall find them yet more severe : wilful impenitent sinners being cut off from the benefits of the new Covenant ; nor barely so, but look'd upon as despisers of it, and that blood of Christ in which it was seal'd ; Heb. 10. 29. nay as those murtherous Wretches that shed it : *They Crucifie to themselves the Son of God afresh* ; Heb. 6. 6.   And this is the fatallest sentence that can fall on any man in this life ; to be thus disfranchised of all the privileges of the Gospel, and rankt as well in punish-ment as guilt, with the most criminous of mankind.

67. F R O M hence 'tis consequent, that the mind remains not only in its native impurity, but in a greater and more incurable one ; whilst that bloud which alone could cleanse it, serves but to embrue and pollute it ; and as it were flush, and excite it to all immanities and vile-nesses:

nesses: and *he that is* thus *filthy*, 'tis the doom pronounc'd against him, that he *shall be filthy still*, Rev. 22. 11.

68. AND then in the second place, what calm can there be to such a mind? what remains to such a person, but that *fearful expectation of wrath and fiery indignation*, which the Apostle mentions, *Heb.* 10. 27? Indeed, were there none but temporal mischiefs to fear, yet it were very unpleasant to think ones self, like *Cain*, out-law'd from the presence and protection of God; to be afraid *that every man that meets us should slay us*, Gen. 4. 14. Nay, those confus'd indistinct fears of indefinite evils which attend guilt, are very unquiet, uneasie inmates in the mind. This is excellently describ'd by *Moses*; *The Lord shall give thee a trembling heart, and failing of eyes, and sorrow of mind, and thy life shall hang in doubt before thee, and thou shalt fear day and night; in the morning thou shalt say, would God it were evening, and in the evening, would God it were morning*, Deut. 28. 65, 66, 67.

69. AND what can be more wretched than to have a mind thus agitated and tost, rackt and tortur'd; especially when thro' all these clouds it sees a glimpse of the eternal Tophet; and knows, that from the billows of this uneasie state, it must be tost into that Lake of fire. And this is indeed *the dregs of*

O   *the*

the cup of Gods wrath, the dreadfulleft and moft aftonifhing of all Scripture denunciations. This comprehends all that the nature of man is capable of fuffering. Divines diftinguifh it into the pain of fenfe, and of lofs: that of fenfe is reprefented to us in Scripture by fire; and that accended, and render'd noifom as well as painful by brimftone, that afflicts the fmell as well as the touch; fometimes by *outer darknefs, wailing and gnafhing of teeth*, to grate the ears, and confume the eyes; by intolerable thirft, to torment the palate. Not that we are to think the fenfitive pains of Hell do not infinitely exceed all thefe; but becaufe thefe are the higheft meafures our prefent capacities can make, and are adequate to thofe fenfes for whofe carnal fatisfactions we incur them.

70. THE pain of lofs is yet more difmal; as being feated in the Soul, whofe fpiritual nature will then ferve it only to render its torments more refin'd, and acute. With what anguifh will it then fee it felf banifh'd from the prefence of God; and confequently from all that may give fatisfaction and blifs to the creature? But yet with how much deeper anguifh will it reflect on it felf as the Author of that deprivation? How will it recollect the many defpis'd tenders of grace, the eafie terms on which falvation might have bin had? And how fadly will confcience then revenge all its

ftifled

ftifled admonitions by an unfilenceable clamor, *that worm which never dies*, Mar. 9. 48., How wounding will it then be *to fee* Abraham, Ifaac *and* Jacob, and all the Saints *in the Kingdom of God*, Luk. 13. 28. (nay, that poor *Lazarus* whom here men turn'd over to the charity of their dogs) and it felf in the company of the devil and his angels, who will then upbraid what they once intic'd to?

71. NATURE abhors nothing more than to have our mifery infulted over by thofe who drew us into it : yet that no circumftance may be lacking to their torment, this muft be the perpetual entertainment of damn'd fouls. And to all this, Eternity is the difmal adjunct ; which is of all other circumftances the moft difconfolate, as leaving not fo much as a glimpfe of hopes ; which here ufes ftill to be the referve, and laft refort of the miferable.

72. THIS Eternity is that which gives an edge, infufes a new acrimony into the torments : and is the higheft ftrain, the vertical point of mifery. Thefe are thofe *terrors of the Lord*, with which the Scripture acquaints us : and fure we cannot fay that thefe are flat contemptible menaces ; but fuch as fuit the dreadful Majefty of that *God who is a confuming fire*, Heb. 12. 29. So that thefe are as aptly accommodated for the exciting our dread, as the promifes were of our love:

O 2

both

both jointly concur to awaken our industry.

73. F O R God has bin so good to mankind, as make the threats conditional as well as the promises: so that we as well know the way to avoid the one, as we do to attain the other. Nor has he any other intendment or end in proposing them, but that we may do so. See to this purpose, with what solemnity he protests it by *Moses*; *I call heaven and earth to record against you this day that I have set before you life and death, blessing and cursing; therefore chuse life, that both thou and thy seed may live,* Deut. 30. 19.

74. I have now run thro' the several parts of Scripture I proposed to speak of. And tho' I have in each given rather short instances and essay's than an exact description, yet even in these contracted lineaments the exquisit proportions may be discern'd. And if the Reader shall hence be incourag'd to extend his contemplations, and as he reads Holy Scripture, observe it in all its graces, and full dimensions; I doubt not he will pronounce from his experience, that the matter of the Divine Book is very correspondent to the Author: which is the highest Eulogy imaginable.

75. I N the next place we are to consider the Holy Scripture in relation to its end and design; in proportion to which every thing is more or less valuable. The most exquisit
frame

frame, and curious contrivance, that has no determinate end or ufe, is but a piece of induftrious folly, a *Spiders web*, as the Prophet fpeaks, *If.* 59. 5. Now thofe defigns have always been efteem'd the moft excellent that have had the moft worthy fubjects, and bin of the greateft extent. Accordingly, thofe who have projected the obliging and benefiting of other men (tho' but within a private Sphere) have always bin lookt on as men of generous and noble defigns. Thofe who have taken their level higher, and directed their aim to a more publick good, tho' but of a City or Nation, have proportionably acquired a greater efteem. But thofe who have afpired to be univerfal benefactors, to do fomething for the common benefit of the world, their fame has commonly reach'd as far as their influence; men have reverenc'd, nay fometimes (according to the common exceffes of mans nature) ador'd them. Many of the Heathen deities (efpecially their demi-gods) having bin only thofe perfons, who by introducing fome ufeful Art, or other part of knowledge, had oblig'd mankind. So we fee what a natural gratitude men are apt to pay to worthy and generous defigns. And if we will be content but to ftand to this common award of our nature, the Scripture will have the faireft claim imaginable to our reverence and thankfulnefs, upon this very account of the excellency of its defigns. 76. N o r

76. Nor need we borrow the balance of the Sanctuary to weigh them in, we may do it in our own scales; for they exactly answer the two properties above mention'd, of profit and diffusiveness which in secular concerns are the standard rules of good designs. For first, it is the sole scope and aim of Scripture, the very end for which 'twas writ, to benefit and advantage men; and that secondly, not only some small select number, some little angle or corner of the world, but the whole race of mankind, the entire Universe; and he that can imagine a more diffusive design, must imagine more worlds also.

77. Now for the first of these, that it is the design of the Scripture to benefit men, we need appeal but to Scripture it self; which surely can give the best account to what ends 'tis directed; and that tells us, it *is to make us wife unto Salvation*, 2 Tim. 3. 15. In which is comprehended the greatest benefit that mans nature is capable of: the making us wise while we live here, and the saving us eternally. And this sure is the most generous, the most obliging design, that 'tis possible even for the Creator to have upon the creature: and this is it which the Holy Scripture negotiates with us.

78. And first, the making us wise, is so inviting a proposal to humanity, that we see when that was much wiser than now it is, it
caught

caught at a fallacious tender of it ; the very sound of it, tho' out of the devils mouth, fascinated our first Parents, and hurried them to the highest disobedience, and certainest ruin. And therefore now God by the Holy Scriptures makes us an offer as much more safe, as it is more sincere ; when he sends his Word thus to be *a lamp to our feet, and a light to our paths,* Pf. 119. 105. to teach us all that is good for us to know, our affectation of ignorance will be more culpable than theirs of knowledge, if we do not admire the kindness, and embrace the bounty of such a tender.

79. N o w the making us wise must be understood according to the Scripture notion of wisdom, which is *not the wisdom of this world, nor the Princes of this world, which come to nought,* as the Apostle speaks, 1 *Cor.* 2. 6. *but that wisdom which descends from above,* Ja. 3. 17. which he there describes to be *first pure, then peaceable, gentle and easie to be intreated, full of mercy and good fruits, without partiality, and without hypocrisie.* Indeed the Scripture usually comprehends these and all other graces under Wisdom ; for it makes it synonymous to that which includes them all, *viz.* the fear of the Lord. Thus we find thoughout the whole Book of Proverbs these us'd as terms convertible. In short, Wisdom is that practical knowledge of God and our selves which engages us to obedience and duty ; and this is agreeable

to

to that definition the Wife man gives of it; *The wisdom of the prudent is to understand his way,* Pro. 14. 8. Without this, all the moft refin'd and aerial fpeculations, are but like *Thales's* ftar-gazing; which fecur'd him not from falling in the water; nay, betray'd him to it. In this is all folid wifdom compris'd.

80. THE utmoft all the wife men in the world have pretended to, is but to know what true happinefs is, and what is the means of attaining it: and what they fought with fo much ftudy, and fo little fuccefs, the Scripture prefents us with in the greateft certainty, and plaineft characters, fuch as *he that runs may read,* Hab. 2. 2. It acquaints us with that fupreme felicity, that chief good whereof Philofophy could only give us a name, and it fhews us the means, marks out a path which will infallibly lead us to it. Accordingly we find that *Solomon* after all the accurate fearch he had made to find *what was that good for the fons of men;* he fhuts up his inqueft in this plain conclufion: *Fear God and keep his commandments; for God fhall bring every work unto judgment,* Eccl. 12. 13, 14. The regulating our lives fo by the rules of Piety, as may acquit us at our final account, is the moft eligible thing that falls within human cognizance; and that not only in relation to the fuperlative happinefs of the next world, but even to the quiet and tranquillity of this. For alas, we

we are impotent giddy creatures, sway'd sometimes by one paffion, fometimes by another; nay often the interfering of our appetites makes us irrefolute which we are to gratifie, whilft in the interim their ftrugling agitates and turmoils the mind. And what can be more defirable in fuch a cafe, than to put our felves under a wifer conduct than our own; and as oppreft States ufe to defeat all leffer pretenders by becoming homagers to fome more potent: fo for us to deliver our felves from the tyranny of our lufts, by giving up our obedience to him whofe fervice is perfect freedom.

81. WERE there no other advantage of the exchange, but the bringing us under fixt and determinate Laws, 'twere very confiderable. Every man would gladly know the terms of his fubjection, and have fome ftanding rule to guide himfelf by ; and Gods Laws are fo, we may certainly know what he requires of us : but the mandates of our paffions are arbitrary and extemporary : what pleafes them to day difgufts them to morrow ; and we muft always be in readinefs to do we know not what, and of all the Arbitrary governments that men either feel or fear, this is doubtlefs the moft miferable. I wifh our apprehenfions of it were but as fenfible : and then we fhould think the Holy Scripture did us the office of a Patriot, in offering us a refcue from fo vile a flavery.

82. AND that it do's make us this offer, is
P

manifeft

manifeſt by the whole tenour of the Bible. For firſt it rowzes and awakes us to a ſenſe of our condition, ſhews us that what we call liberty, is indeed the ſaddeſt ſervitude ; that *he that committeth ſin is the ſervant of ſin*, Jo. 8. 34. that thoſe vices which pretend to ſerve and gratifie us, do really ſubdue and enſlave us, and fetter when they ſeem to embrace : and whereas the will in all other oppreſſions retains its liberty, this tyranny brings that alſo into vaſſallage : renders our ſpirits ſo mean and ſervile, that we chuſe bondage ; are apt to ſay with the Iſraelites, *Let us alone that we may ſerve the Egyptians*, Ex. 14. 12.

83. AND what greater kindneſs can be done for people in this forlorn abject condition, than to animate them to caſt off this yoke, and recover their freedom. And to this are moſt of the Scripture exhortations addreſt ; as may be ſeen in a multitude of places, particularly in the ſixth chapter to the *Romans*, the whole ſcope whereof is directly to this purpoſe.

84. NOR do's it only ſound the alarm, put us upon the conteſt with our enemies, but it aſſiſts us in it, furniſhes us with that *whole armor of God* which we find deſcrib'd, *Eph.* 6. 13. Nay further, it excites our courage, by aſſuring us that if we will not baſely ſurrender our ſelves, we can never be overpower'd ; if we do but ſtand our ground, reſiſt our enemy, he

will

will fly from us ; Ja. 4. 7. And to that purpose
it directs us under what banner we are to lift
our selves; even his who *hath spoil'd principali-
ties and powers*, Col. 2. 15. to whose conduct
and discipline if we constantly adhere, we
cannot miss of victory.

85. A N D then lastly it sets before us the
prize of this conquest ; that we shall not only
recover our liberty, manumit our selves from
the vilest bondage to the vilest and cruellest
oppressors ; but we shall be crown'd for it too,
be rewarded for being kind to our selves, and
be made happy eternally hereafter for being
willing to be happy here.

86. A N D sure these are terms so apparent-
ly advantageous, that he must be infinitly stupid (foolish to destruction) that will not be
thus made wise unto salvation, that despises
or cavils at this divine Book, which means
him so much good, which designs to make
him live here generously and according to the
dignity of his nature, and in the next world
to have that nature sublimated and exalted,
made more capacious of those refin'd and im-
mense felicities, which there await all who
will qualifie themselves for them ; *who* (as the
Apostle speaks) *by patient continuance in well
doing seek for glory, and honour, and immortality, eternal life*, Rom. 2. 7.

87. B U T besides the greatest and principal
advantages which concern our spiritual inte-

rest,

rest, it takes in also the care of our secular, directs us to such a managery of our selves, as is naturally apt to promote a quiet and happy life. Its injunction to live peaceably with all men, keeps us out of the way of many misadventures, which turbulent unruly spirits meet with, and so secures our peace. So also as to wealth, it puts us into the fairest road to riches by prescribing diligence in our callings : what is thus got being like sound flesh, which will stick by us ; whereas the hasty growth of ill-gotten wealth is but a tumour and impostume, which the bigger it swells, the sooner it bursts and leaves us lanker than before. In like manner it shews us also how to guard our reputation, by *providing honest things not only in the sight of God, but also in the sight of men*, 2 Cor. 8. 21. *by abstaining even from all appearance of evil*, 1 Thes. 5. 22. and *making our light shine before men*, Mat. 5. 16. It provides too for our ease and tranquillity, supersedes our anxious cares and sollicitudes, by directing us to *cast our burden upon the Lord*, Ps. 55. 22. and by a reliance on his providence how to secure to our selves all we really want. Finally it fixes us in all the changes, supports us under all the pressures, comforts us amidst all the calamities of this life, by assuring us they shall *all work together for good to those that love God*; Ro. 8. 28.

88. NOR do's the Scripture design to promote

mote our interests consider'd only singly and personally, but also in relation to Societies and Communities; it gives us the best rules of distributive and commutative Justice; teaches us to *render to all their dues*, Rom. 13. 7. to keep our words, to observe inviolably all our pacts and contracts; nay tho' *they prove to our damage*, Psa. 15. 4. and to preserve exact fidelity and truth; which are the sinews of human commerce. It infuses into us noble and generous principles, to prefer a common good before our private: and that highest flight of Ethnic vertue, that of dying for ones Country, is more than the Scripture prescribes even for our common brethren, 1 *Jo.* 3. 16.

89. BUT besides these generals, it descends to more minute directions accommodated to our several circumstances; it gives us appropriate rules in reference to our distinct relations, whether natural, civil, ecclesiastical, or œconomical. And if men would but universally conform to them, to what a blessed harmony would it tune the world? what order and peace would it introduce? There would then be no oppressive Governours, nor mutinous Subjects; no unnatural Parents, nor contumacious Children: no idle Shepherds, or straying Flocks: none of those Domestick jars which oft disquiet, and sometimes subvert families: all would be calm and serene; and give us in realty that golden
Age,

Age , whereof the Poets did but dream.

90. T H I S tendency of the Scripture is re-
markably acknowledg'd in all our publick Ju-
dicatories, where before any teftimony is admitted, we caufe the perfon that is to give his
teftimony, firft to lay hold of with his hands,
then with his mouth to kifs the Holy Scriptures : as if it were impoffible for thofe hands,
which held the myfteries of Truth, to be immediately employ'd in working falfe-hood ; or
that thofe lips which had ador'd thofe Holy
Oracles, fhould be polluted with perjuries and
lies. And I fear, the civil Government is exceedingly fhaken at this day in its firmeft foundation, by the little regard is generally had of
the Holy Scriptures, and what is confequent
thereto, the Oaths that are taken upon them.

91. 'T I S true, we are far remov'd from
that ftate which *Efaiah* Prophecied of under
the Gofpel, tho' we have the Bible among us ;
that when *the Law fhould go forth of* Sion, *and
the Word of the Lord from* Jerufalem, *they fhould
beat their fwords into plow-fhares, and their fpears
into pruning-hooks,* Ef. 2. 4. but that is not from
any defect in it, but from our own perverfenefs : *we have it,* but (as the Apoftle fpeaks in
another fenfe) *as if we had it not,* 1 Cor. 7. 29.
We have it (that is, ufe it) to purpofes widely
different from what it means. Some have it as a
Superfedeas to all the duty it injoins ; and fo they
can but cap texts, talk glibly of Scripture, are
not

not at all concern'd to practice it : some have
it as their Arsenal, to furnish them with Wea-
pons, not against their spiritual enemies, but
their secular : applying all the damnatory sentences they there find, to all those to whose
persons or opinions they have prejudice. And
some have it as a Scene of their mirth, a topick
of raillery, dress their profane and scurrilous
jests in its language ; and study it for no other
end but to abuse it. And whilst we treat it at
this vile rate, no wonder we are never the better for it. For alas, what will it avail us to
have the most soveraign Balsom in our possession, if instead of applying it to our wounds,
we trample it under our feet ?

92. BUT tho' we may frustrate the use, we
cannot alter the nature of things. Gods design
in giving us the Scripture was to make us as
happy as our nature is capable of being; and
the Sripture is excellently adapted to this end :
for as to our eternal felicity, all that believe
there is any such state, must acknowledge the
Scripture chalks us out the ready way to it :
not only because 'tis dictated by God who infallibly knows it, but also by its prescribing
those things which are in themselves best ; and
which a sober Heathen would adjudge fittest
to be rewarded. And as to our temporal happiness, I dare appeal to any unprejudic'd
man, whether any thing can contribute more
to the peace and real happiness of mankind,
than

than the univerfal practice of the Scripture rules would do. Would God we would all confpire to make the experiment ; and then doubtlefs, not only our reafon, but our fenfe too would be convinc'd of it.

93. AND as the defign is thus beneficial, fo in the fecond place is it as extenfive alfo. Time was when the Jews had the inclofure of divine Revelation ; when the Oracles of God were their peculiar depofitum, and the *Heathen had not the knowledge of his Laws,* Pf. 147. *ult.* but fince that by the goodnefs of God the *Gentiles are* become *fellow-heirs,* Eph. 3. 6. he hath alfo deliver'd into their hands the deeds and evidences of their future ftate , given them the Holy Scriptures as the exact and authentick regifters of the covenant between God and man, and thefe not to be like the Heathen Oracles appropriated to fome one or two particular places, fo that they cannot be confulted but at the expence of a pilgrimage ; but laid open to the view of all that will believe themfelves concern'd.

94. IT was a large commiffion our Saviour gave his Difciples : *go preach the Gofpel to every creature,* Mar. 16. 15. (which in the narroweft acception muft be the Gentile world) and yet their oral Gofpel did not reach farther than the written : for wherever the Chriftian Faith was planted, the Holy Scriptures were left as the records of it ; nay, as the confervers of it too,

too, the ftanding rule by which all corruptions were to be detected. 'Tis true, the entire Canon of the New Teftament, as we now have it, was not all at once deliver'd to the Church; the Gofpels and Epiftles being fucceffively writ, as the needs of Chriftians, and the encroachment of Hereticks gave occafion: but at laft they became all together the common magazine of the Church, to furnifh arms both defenfive and offenfive. For as the Gofpel puts in our hands the fhield of Faith, fo the Epiftles help us to hold it, that it may not be wrefted out of our hands again, either by the force of perfecution, or the fly infinuations of vice or Herefie.

95. THUS the Apoftles like prudent leaders have beat up the Ambufhes, difcover'd the fnares that were laid for us; and by difcomfiting Satans forlorn hope, that earlieft Set of falfe teachers and corrupt practices which then invaded the Church, have laid a foundation of victory to the fucceeding Ages, if they will but keep clofe to their conduct, adhere to thofe Sacred Writings they have left behind them in every Church for that purpofe.

96. NOW what was there depofited, was defign'd for the benefit of every particular member of that Church. The Bible was not committed (like the *Regalia*, or rarities of a Nation) to be kept under lock and key (and

Q confeconsequently to constitute a profitable office for the keepers) but expos'd like the Brazen Serpent for universal view and benefit : that sacred Book (like the common air) being every mans propriety, yet no mans inclosure: yet there are a generation of men whose eyes have bin evil, because Gods have bin good: who have seal'd up this spring, monopoliz'd the word of Life, and will allow none to partake of it but such persons, and in such proportions as they please to retail it : an attempt very insolent in respect of God, whose purpose they contradict; and very injurious in respect of man, whose advantage they obstruct. The iniquity of it will be very apparent, if we consider what is offer'd in the following Section.

SECT.

SECT. IV.

The Custody of the Holy Scripture is a privilege and right of the Christian Church, and every member of it ; which cannot without impiety to God, and injustice unto it and them, be taken away or impeacht.

BESIDES the keeping of the divine Law, which is obsequious, and imports a due regard to all its Precepts, commonly exprest in Scripture by *keeping the commandments, hearkning to, and obeying the voice of the Lord, walking in his ways, and observing and doing his statutes and his judgments* : there is a possessory keeping it , in reference to our selves and others ; in respect whereof, Almighty God, *Deut.* 6. and elsewhere frequently, having enjoin'd the people of *Israel, to love the Lord their God with all their heart, and with all their soul, and with all their might, and that the words which he commanded them should be in their heart,* he adds, *that they shall teach them diligently to their children, and shall talk of them when they sit down in their houses, and when they walk by the way, and when they lie down, and when they rise up :*

and that they bind them for a sign upon their hand, and that they shall be as frontlets between their eyes, and that they shall write them upon the posts of their house, and on their gates. So justly was the Law call'd the Scripture, being written by them, and worn upon the several parts of the body, inscrib'd upon the walls of their houses, the entrance of their doors, and gates of their Cities; and in a word, placed before their eyes wherever they convers'd.

2. AND this was granted to the Jews, as matter of privilege and favour. *To them*, says Saint *Paul*, Rom. 9. 4. *pertaineth the adoption, and the glory, and the covenants, and the giving of the Law.* And the same Saint *Paul*, at the 3. chap. 2. v. of that Epistle, unto the question, *what advantage hath the Jew, or what profit is there of circumcision*, answers, that it is *much every way, chiefly because unto them were committed the Oracles of God.* This *depositum* or trust was granted to the Fathers, that it should be continued down unto their children. *He made a covenant*, says *David*, Ps. 78. v. 5. *with* Jacob, *and gave* Israel *a Law, which he commanded our Fore-fathers to teach their children, that their posterity might know it, and the children which are yet unborn: to the intent that when they came up, they might shew their children the same.* Which Scripture by a perpetual succession was to be handed down unto the Christian Church; the Apostles on all occasions appeal-

appealing unto them, as being *read in the Synagogues every Sabbath day*, Act. 13. 27. and alſo privately, in their hands; ſo that they might at pleaſure *search into them*, Jo. 5. 39. Act. 17. 11. Hereupon the Jews are by Saint *Auſtin* call'd the *Capſarii*, or ſervants that carried the Chriſtian Books. And *Athanaſius* in his Tract of the Incarnation, ſays, *The Law was not for the Jews only, nor were the Prophets ſent for them alone; but that Nation was the Divinity-School of the whole world; from whence they were to fetch the knowledge of God and the way of ſpiritual living*: which amounts to what the Apoſtle ſays, Galat. 3. 24. *That the Law was a School-maſter to bring us unto Chriſt.*

3. AND 'tis obſervable that the very ſame word, *Rom.* 3. 2. in the Text even now recited, which expreſſes the *committing* of the Oracles of God to the Jews, is made uſe of conſtantly by Saint *Paul*, when he declares the truſt and duty incumbent on him in the preaching of the Goſpel: of which, ſee 1 *Cor.* 9. 17. *Gal.* 2. 7. 1 *Theſ.* 2. 4. 1 *Tim.* 1. 11. *Tit.* 1. 3. And therefore, as he ſays, 1 *Cor.* 9. *Tho' I preach the Goſpel, I have nothing to glory of; for neceſſity is laid upon me, yea, wo is unto me if I preach not the Goſpel, for if I do this thing willingly, I have a reward; but if againſt my will, a diſpenſation of the Goſpel is committed unto me*: So may all Chriſtians ſay; if we our ſelves keep and tranſmit to our poſterities the Holy Scriptures,

ptures, we have nothing to glory of, for a necessity is laid upon us, and wo be unto us if we do not our selves keep, and transmit to our posterity the Holy Scriptures. If we do this thing willingly, we have a reward ; but if against our will, the custody of the Gospel, and at least that dispensation of it, is committed to us. But if we are Traditors, and give up our Bibles, or take them away from others ; let us consider how black an apostacy and sacrilege we shall incur.

4. THE Mosaick Law was a temporary constitution, and only *a shadow of good things to come*, Heb. 10. 1. but the Gospel being in its duration as well as its intendment, *everlasting*, Rev. 14. 6. and to remain *when time shall be no more*, Rev. 10. 6. it is an infinitely more precious *depositum*, and so with greater care and solemner attestation to be preserv'd. Not only the Clergy, or the people of one particular Church, nor the Clergy of the universal are intrusted with this care ; but 'tis the charge, the privilege and duty of every Christian man, that either is, or was, or shall be in the world ; even that collective Church which above all competition, *is the pillar and ground of truth*, 1 Tim. 3. 15. against which the assaults of men and devils, and even the *gates of hell shall not prevail*, Mat. 16. 18.

5. THE Gospels were not written by their Holy Pen-men to instruct the Apostles, but to

the

the Chriftian Church, *that they might believe Jefus was the Chrift, the fon of God, and that believing they might have life thro' his name*, Jo. 20. 31. The Epiftles were not addreft peculiarly to the Bifhops and Deacons, *but all the Holy brethren, to the Churches of God that are fanctified in Jefus Chrift, and to all thofe that call upon the name of the Lord Jefus Chrift*, Rom. 1. 7. 1 Cor. 1. 2. 2 Cor. 1. 1. Galat. 1. 2. Eph. 1. 1. Col. 4. 16. 1 Thef. 5. 27. Phil. 1. 1. Jam. 1. 1. 1 Pet. 1. 1. 2 Pet. 1. Revel. 1. 4. Or if by chance fome one or two of the Epiftles were addreft to an Ecclefiaftick perfon, as thofe to *Timothy* and *Titus*, their purport plainly refers to community of Chriftians, and the *depofitum* committed to their truft ; 1 *Tim.* 6. 20. And Saint *John* on the other fide directs his Epiftles to thofe who were plainly fecular; to fathers, youngmen and little children ; and a Lady and her children, Epift. 1. chap. 2. 12, 13, 14. and Epift. 2. 1. 1.

6. BUT befides the intereft which every Chriftian has in the cuftody of the Scripture upon the account of its being a *depofitum* intrufted to him, he has alfo another no lefs forcible ; that 'tis the Teftament of his Saviour, by which he becomes a Son of God, *no more a Servant but a Son ; and if he be a Son*, it is the Apoftles inference, that he is *then an heir, an heir of God thro' Chrift*, Gal. 4. 7. Now as he who is heir to an eftate, is alfo to the

deeds

deeds and conveiances thereof; which without injury cannot be detain'd, or if they be, there is a remedy at Law for the recovery of them: so it fares in our Christian inheritance: every believer by the privilege of faith, is made a Son of *Abraham,* and an heir of the promises made unto the fathers, whereby he has an hereditary interest in the Old Testament; and also by the privilege of the same Faith he has a firm right to the *purchast possession,* Eph. 1. 14. and the charter thereof, the New. Therefore the detention of the Scriptures, which are made up of these two parts, is a manifest injustice, and sacrilegious invasion of right, which the person wrong'd is impower'd, nay, is strictly oblig'd by all lawful means to vindicate.

7. WHICH invasion of right will appear more flagrant when the nature and importance of it is consider'd; which relating to mens spiritual interest, renders the violation infinitely more injurious than it could be in any secular. I might mention several detriments consequent to this detention of Scripture, even as many as there are benefits appendant to the free use of it; but there is one of so fundamental and comprehensive a nature, that I need name no more; and that is, that it delivers men up to any delusion their teachers shall impose upon them, by depriving them of means of detecting them.
Where

Where there is no standard or measures, 'tis easie for men to falsifie both ; and no less easie is it to adulterate doctrines, where no recourse can be had to the primary rule. Now that there is a possibility that false teachers may arise, we have all assurance ; nay we have the word of Christ, and his Apostles that it should be so : and all Ecclesiastick Story to attest it has bin so. And if in the first and purest times (those Ages of more immediate illumination) the *God of this world* found instruments whereby to *blind mens minds,* 2 Cor. 4. 4. it cannot be suppos'd impossible or improbable he should do so now.

8. B u t to leave generals, and to speak to the case of that Church which magisterially prohibits Scripture to the vulgar : she manifestly stands liable to that charge of our Saviour, Luk. 11. 52. *Ye have taken away the key of knowledge ;* and by allowing the common people no more Scripture than what she affords them in their Sermons and private Manuals, keeps it in her power to impose on them what she pleases. For 'tis sure those portions she selects for them, shall be none of those which clash with the doctrines she recommends : and when ever she will use this power to the corrupting their faith, or worship (yea, or their manners either) they must brutishly submit to it, because they cannot bring her dictates to the test.

R　　　　　　　　　B u t

9. BUT 'twill be said, this danger she wards by her doctrine of infallibility: that is, she enervates a probable supposition attested by event, by an impossible one confuted by event. For 'tis certain that all particular Churches may err ; and tho' the consciousness of that, forces the Roman Church upon the absurd pretence of universality, to assert her infallibility ; yet alas *Tyber* may as well call it self the Ocean, or *Italy* the world, as the Roman Church may name it self the universal ; whilst 'tis so apparent that far the less part of Christians are under her communion. And if she be but a particular Church, she has no immunity from errours, nor those under her from having those errours, (how pernicious soever) impos'd upon them. As to her having actually err'd, and in diverse particulars, the proof of that has bin the work of so many Volumes, that 'twould be impertinent here to undertake it : I shall only instance in that of Image-worship , a practice perfectly irreconcilable with the second commandment ; and doubtless, clearly discern'd by her to be so : upon which account it is, that tho' by Translations and Paraphrases she wrests and moulds other Texts to comply with her doctrins, yet she dares not trust to those arts for this : but takes a more compendious course, and expunges the Commandment ; as is evident in her Catechisms and

other

other Manuals.   Now a Church that can thus
sacrilegiously purloin one Commandment
(and such a one as God has own'd himself the
most jealously concern'd in) and to delude her
Children split another to make up the number, may as her needs require, substract
and divide what others she please : and then
whilst all resort to Scripture is obstructed;
how fatal a hazard must those poor souls run,
who are oblig'd to follow these blind, or rather these winking guides into the ditch?

10. BUT all these criminations she retorts
by objecting the dangers of allowing the Scriptures to the vulgar, which she accuses as the
spring of all Sects, Schisms, and Heresies. To
which I answer first, that supposing this were
true, 'twas certainly foreseen by God, who
notwithstanding laid no restraint; probably
as fore-seeing, that the dangers of implicit
faith (to which such a restraint must subject
men) would be far greater : and if God saw fit
to indulge the liberty, those that shall oppose
it, must certainly think they do not only partake, but have transplanted infallibility from
God to themselves.

11. BUT secondly, 'tis not generally true,
that Sects, Schisms, and Heresies are owing to
this liberty : All Ecclesiastical Story shews us
that they were not the illiterate Lay-men, but
the learned Clarks who were usually the
broachers of Heresies.   And indeed many of

them were so subtile and aerial, as could never have bin forg'd in grosser brains; but were founded not on Scripture merely mistaken, but rackt and distorted with nice criticisms, and quirks of Logick, as several of the Ancients complain: some again sprang from that ambition of attaining, or impatience of missing Ecclesiastical dignities: which appropriates them to the Clergy. So that if the abuse infer a forfeiture of the use, the Learned have of others the least title to the Scriptures; and perhaps those who now ingross them, the least title of all the Learned.

12. On the other side, Church-story indeed mentions some Lay-propugners of Heresies; but those for the most part were either so gross and bestial; as disparag'd and confuted themselves and Authors, and rose rather from the brutish inclination of the men, than from their mistakes of Scripture: or else they were by the immediate infusion of the devil, who backt his Heretical suggestions with sorceries and lying wonders, as in *Simon Magus, Menander, &c.* And for latter times, tho' sometimes there happens among the vulgar a few pragmatick spirits, that love to tamper with the obscurest Texts, and will undertake to expound before they understand; yet that is not their common temper: the generality are rather in the other extreme, stupid and unobservant even of the plainest doctrines. And if

to

to this be objected the multitude of Quakers and Fanaticks, who generally are of the ignorant fort ; I anfwer, that 'tis manifeft the firft propugners of thofe tenets in *Germany* were not feduc'd into them by miftakes of Scripture, but induftrioufly form'd them, at once to difguife and promote their villainous defigns of fedition and rapine: and as for thofe amongfts us, it not at all certain that their firft errours were their own productions: there are vehement prefumptions that the feeds were fown by greater Artificers ; whofe firft bufinefs was to unhinge them from the Church, and then to fill their heads with ftrange Chimera's of their privileges and perfections ; and by that intoxication of fpiritual pride, difpofe them for all delufions : and thereby render them, like *Samfons* Foxes, fit inftruments to fet all in combuftion.

13. B u t admit this were but a conjecture, and that they were the fole Authors of their own frenzy ; how appears it that the liberty of reading the Scriptures was the caufe of it ? Had thefe men bin of the Romifh communion, and fo bin interdicted private reading, yet fome broken parts of Scripture would have bin in Sermons and Books of devotion communicated to them ; had it not bin as poffible for them to have wrefted what they heard as what they read ? In one refpect it feems rather
ther

ther more likely : for in thofe loofe and incidental quotations the connexion is fometimes not fo difcernable : and many Texts there are whofe fenfe is fo interwoven with the context, that without confulting that, there may be very pernicious miftakes : on which account it is probably more fafe that the Auditor fhould have Bibles to confult. So that this reftraint of Scripture is a very fallible expedient of the infallible Church. And indeed themfelves have in event found it fo ; for if it were fo foveraign a prophylactick againft errour, how comes it to pafs that fo many of their members who were under that difcipline have revolted from them into that which they call Herefie ? If they fay, the defection was made by fome of the Learned to whom the Scripture was allow'd, why do they not (according to their way of arguing) take it from them alfo upon that experiment of its mifchief, and confine it only to the infallible chair ? but if they own them to have bin unlearn'd (as probably the Albigenfes and Waldenfes, &c. were) they may fee how infignificant a guard this reftraint is againft errour : and learn how little is got by that policy which controuls the divine Wifdom.

14. NOR can they take fhelter in the example of the primitive Chriftians: for they in the conftant ufe of the Holy Scriptures yielded not unto the Jews. Whereas the Jews had
the

the Scriptures read publickly to them every Sabbath-day ; which *Josephus* against *Appion* thus expresses : *Moses expounded to the Jews the most excellent and necessary learning of the Law ; not by hearing it once or twice, but every seventh-day laying aside their works, he commanded them to assemble for the hearing of the Law, and throughly and exactly to learn it.* Parallel to this was the practice of the primitive Church, perform'd by the Lector, or Reader, of which *Justin Martyr* in his 2. Apol. gives this account. *On the day call'd Sunday, all that abide in towns or the countries about, meet in one place, and the writings of the Apostles and Prophets are read, so far as there is place.* So *Tertullian* in his *Apol.* describing the offices in the publick Assemblies : *We feed our faith with the sacred Words, we raise our hopes, and establish our reliance.*

15. And as the Jews thought it indecent for persons professing piety, to let three days pass without the offices thereof in the congregation ; and thefore met in their Synagogues upon every Tuesday and Thursday in the week, and there perform'd the duties of fasting, prayer, and hearing the Holy Scriptures ; concerning which is the boast of the Pharisee, *Luk.* 18. 12. in conformity hereto the Christians also, their Sabbath being brought forward from the Saturday to the day following ; that the like number of days might not pass them without performing the aforesaid

said duties in the congregation; met together on the Wednesdays and Frydays, which were the days of Station, so frequently mention'd in *Tertullian*, and others, the first writers of the Church. *Tertullian* expresly says, that the Christians dedicated to the offices of Piety, *the fourth and sixth-day of the week* : and *Clemens Alex.* says of the Christians, that *they understood the secret reasons of their weekly fasts, to wit, those of the fourth-day of the week, and that of preparation before the Sabbath ; commonly call'd Wednesday and Friday.* Where, by the way, we may take notice what ground there is for the observation of the Wednesday and Friday in our Church, and the Litanies then appointed, so much neglected in this profligate Age.

16. BUT secondly, as the Jews were diligent in the private reading of the Scripture; being taught it from their infancy : which custom Saint *Paul* refers to 1 *Tim.* 3. 15. whereof *Josephus* against *Appion* says, *That if a man ask any Jew concerning the Laws, he will tell every thing readier than his name : for learning them from the first time they have sense of any thing, they retain them imprinted in their minds.* So were the first Christians equally industrious in improving their knowledge of divine Truth. *The whole life of a Christian:* says *Clem. Alex. Strom. l. 7. is a Holy solemnity, there his sacrifices are prayers and praises; be-*

fore

fore every meal he has the readings of the Holy Scriptures; and Psalms, and Hymns at the time of his meals. Which *Tertullian* also describes in his Apol. and Saint *Cyprian* in the end of the Epist. to *Donatus*.

17. AND this is farther evidenc'd by the early and numerous versions of the Scriptures into all vulgar Languages; concerning which *Theodoret* speaks in his Book of the Cure of the Affections of the Greeks, Serm. 5. *We Christians* (says he) *are enabled to shew the power of Apostolick and Prophetick Doctrines, which have fill'd all Countries under Heaven. For that which was formerly utter'd in Hebrew, is not only translated into the Language of the Grecians, but also the Romans, Egyptians, Persians, Indians, Armenians, Scythians, Samaritans; and in a word into all the Languages that are us'd by any Nation.* The same is said by Saint *Chrysostom* in his first Homily upon Saint *John*.

18. NOR was this done by the blind zeal of inconsiderable men, but the most eminent Doctors of the Church were concern'd herein: such as *Origen*, who with infinite labour contriv'd the Hexapla. Saint *Chrysostom*, who translated the New Testament, Psalms, and some part of the Old Testament into the Armenian Tongue, as witnesses *Geor. Alex.* in the life of *Chrysost.* So *Ulphilas* the first Bishop of the Goths translated the Holy Scripture into the Gothic; as *Socrat. Eccl. Hist. l. 4. cap. 33.*

S

and

and others testifie. Saint *Jerom,* who translated them not only into Latin from the Hebrew, the Old Italick version having bin from
the Greek ; but also into his native vulgar
Dalmatick : which he says himself in his Epistle to *Sophronius.*

19. BUT the peoples having them for their
private and constant use, appears farther by
the Heathens making the extorting of them
a part of their persecution : and when divers
did faint in that trial, and basely surren-
der'd them, we find the Church level'd her
severity only against the offending persons,
did not (according to the Romish equity) pu-
nish the Innocent, by depriving them of
that Sacred Book, because the others had so
unworthily prostituted it (tho' the preven-
tion of such a profanation for the future had
bin as fair a plea for it as the Romanists do
now make:) but on the contrary the primitive Fathers are frequent, nay indeed importunate in their exhortations to the private study of Holy Scripture, which they recommend
to Christians of all Ranks, Ages, and Sexes.

20. As an instance hereof let us hear *Clemens* of *Alex.* in his Exhort. *The word,* says
he, *is not hid from any, it is a common light
that shineth to all men ; there is no obscurity in
it ; hear it you that be far off, and hear it you that
are nigh.*

21. To this purpose St. *Jerom* speaks in his
Epistle

Epiftle to *Leta*, whom he directs in the education of her young daughter, and advifes, *that inftead of gems and filk, fhe be enamour'd with the Holy Scripture; wherein not gold, or skins, or Babylonian embroideries, but a correct and beautiful variety producing faith, will recommend its felf.* Let her firft learn the Pfalter, *and be entertain'd with thofe fongs; then be inftructed unto life by the Proverbs of* Solomon : *let her learn from* Ecclefiaftes *to defpife worldly things; tranfcribe from* Job *the practice of patience and vertue : let her pafs then to the Gofpels, and never let them be out of her hands : and then imbibe with all the faculties of the mind, the Acts of the Apoftles, and Epiftles.* When *fhe has enrich'd the ftorehoufe of her breaft with thefe treafures, let her learn the Prophets, the Heptateuch, or books of* Mofes, Jofhua *and* Judges, *the books of* Kings *and* Chronicles, *the volumes of* Ezra *and* Efther*; and laftly the* Canticles. And indeed, this Father is fo concern'd to have the unletter'd female fex skilful in the Scriptures, that tho' he fharply rebukes their pride and overweening; he not only frequently refolves their doubts concerning difficult places in the faid Scriptures, but dedicates feveral of his Commentaries to them.

22. The fame is to be faid of Saint *Auftin,* who in his Epiftles to unletter'd Laicks, encourages their enquiries concerning the Scripture, affuring *Volufianus* Ep. 3. *that it fpeaks*

thofe

those things that are plain to the heart of the learned and unlearned, as a familiar friend; in the mysterious, mounts not up into high phrases which might deter a slow and unlearned mind, (as the poor are in their addresses to the rich;) but invites all with lowly speech, feeding with manifest truth, and exercising with secret. And *Ep.* 1. 21. tells the devout *Proba*, that *in this world, where we are absent from the Lord, and walk by faith and not by sight, the soul is to think it self desolate, and never cease from praier, and the words of divine and holy Scripture,* &c.

23. S A I N T *Chrysostom* in his third Homily of *Lazarus* thus addresses himself to *married persons, house-holders, and people engag'd in trades and secular professions*; telling them, *that the reading of the Scripture is a great defensative against sin; and on the other side, the ignorance thereof is a deep and head-long precipice; that not to know the Law of God, is the utter loss of salvation; that this has caus'd heresies, and corruption of life, and has confounded the order of things: for it cannot be by any means, that his labor should be fruitless, who emploies himself in a daily and attentive reading of the Scripture.*

24. *I am not,* saies the same St. *Chry. Hom.* 9. on *Colos.* 3. *a Monk, I have wife and children, and the cares of a family. But 'tis a destructive opinion, that the reading of the Scripture pertains only to those who have addicted themselves to a monastick life; when the reading of Scripture*

is

is much more necessary for secular persons: for they who converse abroad, and receive frequent wounds, are in greatest need of remedies and preservatives. So Hom. 2. on Mat. *Hearken all you that are secular, how you ought to order your wives and children; and how you are particularly enjoin'd to read the Scriptures, and that not perfunctorily, or by chance, but very diligently.*

25. LIKEWISE *Hom.* 3. on *Laz. What saiest thou, O man? it is not thy business to turn over the Scripture, being distracted by innumerable cares; no, thou hast therefore the greater obligation: others do not so much stand in need of the aids of the Scripture, as they who are conversant in much business.* Farther, *Hom.* 8. on *Heb.* 5. *I beseech you neglect not the reading of the Scriptures; but whether we comprehend the meaning of what is spoken or not, let us alwaies be conversant in them: for daily meditation strengthens the memory; and it frequently happens, that what you now cannot find out, if you attempt it again, you will the next day discover: for God of his goodness will enlighten the mind.* It were endless to transcribe all the Exhortations of the ancient Doctors and Fathers of the Church; they not only permitted, but earnestly prest upon all Christians, whatever their estate or condition were, the constant reading of the holy Scripture. Nor indeed was their restraint ever heard of till the Church of *Rome* had espous'd such doctrines as would

not

not bear the teſt of Scripture: and then as
thoſe who deal in falſe wares are us'd to do,
they found it neceſſary to proportion their
lights accordingly.

26. This *Peter Sutor* in his ſecond Book
cap. 22. of the Tranſlation of the Scripture
honeſtly confeſſes, ſaying, *that whereas many
things are enjoin'd which are not expreſly in Scripture, the unlearned obſerving this, will be apt
to murmur and complain that ſo heavy burthens
are laid upon them, and their Chriſtian liberty
infring'd. They will eaſily be with-drawn from
obſerving the Conſtitutions of the Church, when
they find that they are not contain'd in the
Law of Chriſt.* And that this was not a frivolous ſuggeſtion, the deſperate attemt of the
Romaniſts above mention'd, in leaving out
the ſecond Commandment in their Primers
and Catechiſms which they communicate to
the people, may paſs for an irrefragable evidence; For what Lay-man would not be
ſhockt, to find Almighty God command, *not to
make any graven image, nor the likeneſs of any
thing that is in heaven above, or in the earth be-
neath, or in the water under the earth; that no one
ſhould bow down to them, nor worſhip them:* when
he ſees the contrary is practic'd and commanded by the Church.

27. But would God none but the Ro-
maniſt were impeachable of this detention
of Scripture: there are too many among us
that

that are thus falſe and envious to themſelves:
and what the former do upon policy and pretence of reverence, thoſe do upon mere oſci-
tancy and avow'd profaneſs; which are much
worſe inducements.   And for ſuch as theſe to
declaim againſt detention of the Scripture, is
like the Law-ſuits of thoſe who contend only
about ſuch little punctilio's as themſelves deſign no advantage from, but only the worſting
their Adverſaries: and it would be much ſafer
for them to lie under the interdict of others,
than thus to reſtrain themſelves: even as much
as the errors of obedience are more excuſable,
than thoſe of contemt and profaneſs.

28. And here I would have it ſeriouſly
conſider'd that the Edict of *Diocletian* for
the demoliſhing the Chriſtian Churches, and
the burning their Bibles; became the character and particular aggravation of his moſt
bloudy perſecution.   Now ſhould Almighty
God call us to the like trial, ſhould Antichri-
ſtian violence, whether heathen or other, take
from us our Churches and our Bibles, what
comfort could we have in that calamity, if
our contemt of thoſe bleſſings drove them
from us; nay, prevented perſecution, and be-
reft us of them even whilſt we had them in
our power? He who neglects to make his
conſtant reſort unto the Church, which by
Gods mercy now ſtands open; or to read diligently the holy Scriptures, which by the
ſame

ſame divine Goodneſs are free for him to uſe, is his own *Diocletian*; and without the terrors of death, or torments, has renounc'd, if not the Faith, the great inſtruments of its conveiance, and pledge of God Almighties preſence among the ſons of men.

29. BUT what if men either upon the one motive or the other, will not read; yet the Srriptures continue ſtill moſt worthy to be read: they retain ſtill their propriety for all thoſe excellent ends to which God deſign'd them : and as the Prophet tells the Jews, *Ez. 2. 5. whether they will hear, or whether they will forbear, they ſhall know that there has bin a Prophet among them* : ſo whether we will take the benefit or no, we ſhall one day find that the holy Scriptures would have made us *wiſe unto ſalvation.* If thro our fault alone they fail to do ſo, they will one day aſſume a leſs grateful office; and from guides and aſſiſtants, become accuſers and witneſſes againſt us.

SECT.

SECT. V.

The Scripture has great propriety and fitness towards the attainment of its excellent end.

WE are now in the next place to consider how exactly the holy Scriptures are adapted to those great ends to which they are directed: how sufficient they are for that important negotiation on which they are sent: and that we shall certainly find them, if we look on them either intrinsecally, or circumstantially. For the first of these notions we need only to reflect on the third Part of this discourse, where the Scripture in respect of the subject Matter is evinc'd to be a system of the most excellent Laws, backt with the most transcendent rewards and punishments; and the certainty of those confirm'd by such pregnant instances of Gods mercies and vengeance in this world, as are the surest gages and earnests of what we are bid to expect in another.

2. Now what method imaginable can there be used to rational creatures of more force and energy? Nay it seems to descend

T   even

even to our paſſions and accommodates it
ſelf to our ſeveral inclinations.   And ſeeing
how few Proſelytes there are to bare and naked
vertue, and how many to intereſt and advantage ; God cloſes with them upon their own
terms, and does not ſo much injoin as buy thoſe
little ſervices he asks from us.

3. B u t becauſe ſome mens natures are ſo
diſingenuous as to hate to be oblig'd no leſs
than to be reform'd, the Scripture has goads
and ſcourges to drive ſuch beaſts as will not
be led ; terrors and threatnings, and thoſe
of moſt formidable ſorts, to affright thoſe
who will not be allur'd.   Nay left incredulous men ſhould queſtion the reality of future
rewards or puniſhments, the Scripture gives as
ſenſible evidence of them as we are capable
of receiving in this world; by regiſtring ſuch
ſignal protections and judgments proportion'd to vertue and vice, as ſufficiently atteſts
the Pſalmiſts Axiom: *Doubtleſs there is a God
that judgeth the earth,* Pſal. 58. 11. and leaves
nothing to the impenitent ſinner, but a *fearful
expeEtation of that fiery indignation* threatned
hereafter ; *Heb.* 10. 27.

4. A n d now methinks the Scripture ſeems to
be that *net* our Saviour ſpeaks of, *that caught of
every ſort,* Mat. 13. 47. it is of ſo vaſt a com-
paſs, that it muſt, one would think, fetch in all
kind of tempers: and ſure had we not mixt natures with fiends, contracted ſo me of their malice

lice and obstinacy, mere human pravity could not hold out.

5. And as the holy Scripture is thus fitly proportion'd to its end in respect of the subject matter, so is it also in reference to its circumstances, which all conspire to render it, *the power of God unto salvation,* Rom. 1. 16. In the first rank of those we must place its divine original, which stamps it with an uncontroulable autority; and is an infallible security that the matter of it is perfectly true: since it proceeds from that essential verity which cannot abuse us with fraudulent promises or threatnings: and from that infinite power that cannot be impeded in the execution of what he purposes.

6. Yet to render this circumstance efficacious there needs another; to wit, that its being the word of God be sufficiently testifi'd to us: and we have in the fore-going discourse evinced it to be so; and that in the utmost degree that a matter of that kind is capable of, beyond which no sober man will require evidence in any thing. And certainly these two circumstances thus united, have a mighty force to impress the dictates of Scripture on us. And we must rebel against God and our own convictions too, to hold out against it.

7. A third circumstance relates to the frame and composure of this divine Book,

both

both as to method, and ſtile: concerning which I have already made ſome reflexions. But now that I may ſpeak more diſtinctly, I obſerve it takes its riſe from the firſt point of time wherein 'twas poſſible for mankind to be concern'd; and ſo gradually proceeds to its fall and renovation: ſhews us firſt our need of a Redeemer, and then points us out who it is by types and promiſes in the Old Teſtament, and by way of hiſtory and completion in the New. In the former it acquaints us with that pedagogy of the Law which God deſign'd as our *Schole-maſter to bring us to Chriſt*, Gal. 3. 25. and in the Goſpel ſhews us yet a more excellent way; preſents us with thoſe more ſublime elevated doctrines, which Chriſt came down from heaven to reveal.

8. As for the ſtile, that is full of grateful variety, ſometimes high and majeſtick, as becomes that *high and holy one that inhabiteth eternity*, Eſai. 57. 15. and ſometimes ſo humble and after the manner of men, as agrees to the other part of his Character, *his dwelling is with him that is of an humble ſpirit*, Eſay. 57. 15. I know profane wits are apt to brand this as an unevenneſs of ſtile: but they may as well accuſe the various notes of Muſick as deſtructive to harmony, or blame an Orator for being able to tune his tongue to the moſt different ſtrains.

9. Ano-

9. ANOTHER excellency of the ftile, is its propriety to the feveral fubjects it treats of. When it fpeaks of fuch things as God would not have men pry into, it wraps them up in clouds and thick darknefs; by that means to deter inquifitive man (as he did at *Sinai*) from breaking into the mount, *Ex.* 20. And that he gives any intimation at all of fuch, feems defign'd only to give us a juft eftimate how fhallow our comprehenfions are; and excite us to adore and admire that Abyfs of divine Wifdom which we can never fathom.

10. THINGS of a middle nature, which may be ufeful to fome, but are not indifpenfibly neceflary to all, the Scripture leaves more acceffible; yet not fo obvious as to be within every mans reach: but makes them only the prize of induftry, praier, and humble endeavors. And it is no fmall benefit, that thofe who covet the knowledge of divine Truth, are by it engag'd to take thefe vertues in the way. Befides there is fo much time requir'd to that ftudy, as renders it inconfiftent with thofe fecular bufineffes wherein the generality of men are immerft: and confequently 'tis neceflary that thofe who addict themfelves to the one, have competent vacancy from the other: And in this it hath a vifible ufe by being very contributive to the mantaining that fpiritual fubordination of the

people

people to the Pastors; which God has establish'd. *Miriam* and *Corahs* Partisans are a pregnant instance how much the opinion of equal knowledge unfits for subjection: and we see by sad experience how much the bare pretence of it has disturb'd the Church, and made those turn preachers who never were understanding hearers.

11. BUT besides these more abstruse, there are easier truths in which every man is concern'd; the explicit knowledg whereof is necessary to all: I mean the divine Rules for saving Faith and Manners. And in those the Scripture stile is as plain as is possible: condescends to the apprehensions of the rudest capacities: so that none that can read the Scripture but will there find the way to bliss evidently chalk'd out to him. That I may use the words of Saint *Gregory, the Lamb may wade in those waters of Life, as well as the Elephant may swim.* The Holy Ghost, as St. *Austin* tells us, lib. 2. of Christian doctrine, cap. 6. *has made in the plainer places of Scripture magnificent and healthful provision for our hunger; and in the obscure, against satiety. For there are scarce any things drawn from obscure places, which in others are not spoken most plainly.* And he farther adds, *that if any thing happen to be no where explain'd, every man may there abound in his own sense.*

12. So again, in the same Book, cap. 9. he

he faies, *that all thofe things which concern Faith and Manners, are plainly to be met with in the Scripture*: and Saint *Jerom* in his Comment on *Ef.* 19. tells us, *that 'tis the cuftom of the Scripture to clofe obfcure fayings with thofe that are eafy; and what was firft expreft darkly, to propofe in evident words*: which very thing is faid likewife by Saint *Chryfoftom, Hom.* 9. 2 *Cor.* 4. 11. who in his firft Homily on St. *Mat.* farther declares, *that the Scriptures are eafy to be underftood, and expos'd to vulgar capacities.*

13. HE faies again, Hom. upon *Efay, that the Scriptures are not mettals that require the help of Miners, but afford a treafure eafily to be had to them that feek the riches contain'd in them. It is enough only to ftoop down, and look upon them, and depart replenifh'd with wealth; it is enough only to open them, and behold the fplendor of thofe Gems.* Again Hom. 3. on the fecond Ep. to the Theff. 2. *All things are evident and ftrait, which are in the holy Scripture; whatever is neceffary is manifeft.* So alfo Hom. 3. on Gen. 14. *It cannot be that he who is ftudious in the holy Scripture fhould be rejetted: for tho the inftruction of men be wanting, the Lord from above will inlighten our minds, fhine in upon our reafon, reveal what is fecret, and teach what we do not know.* So Hom. 1. on Jo. 11. *Almighty God involves his doctrine with no mifts, and darknefs, as did the Philofophers: his doctrine*

ſtrine is brighter than the Sun-beams, and more illuſtrious ; and therefore every where diffus'd : and Hom. 6. on Jo. 11. *His doctrine is ſo facile, that not only the wiſe, but even women, and youths muſt comprehend it.* Hom. 13. on Gen. 2. *Let us go to the Scripture as our Mark, which is its own interpreter.* And ſoon after ſaies, that *the Scripture interprets it ſelf, and ſuffers not its Auditor to err.* To the ſame purpoſe ſaies *Cyril* in his third book againſt *Julian. In the Scripture nothing is difficult to them, who are converſant in them as they ought to be.*

14. IT is therefore a groundleſs cavil which men make at the obſcurity of the Scripture ; ſince it is not obſcure in thoſe things wherein 'tis our common intereſt it ſhould be plain : which ſufficiently juſtifies its propriety to that great end of *making us wiſe unto Salvation.* And for thoſe things which ſeem leſs intelligible to us, many of them become ſo, not by the innate obſcurity of the Text, but by extrinſic circumſtances (of which perhaps the over-buſy tampering of Paraphraſts, pleaſed with new notions of their own, may be reckon'd for one.) But this ſubject the Reader may find ſo well purſued in Mr. *Boyls* Tract concerning the ſtile of Scripture, that I ſhall be kindeſt both to him and it to refer him thither ; as alſo for anſwer to thoſe other querulous objections which men galled with the ſenſe of the Scripture, have made to its ſtile.

15. A

15. A third circumstance in which the Scripture is fitted to attain its end, is its being committed to writing, as that is distinguish'd from oral delivery.   It is most true, the word of God is of equal autority and efficacy which way soever it be deliver'd: The Sermons of the Apostles were every jot as divine and powerful out of their mouths, as they are now in their story.   All the advantage therefore that the written Word can pretend to, is in order to its perpetuity, as it is a securer way of derivation to posterity, than that of oral Tradition.   To evince that it is so, I shall first weigh the rational probabilities on either side.   Secondly, I shall consider to which God himself appears in Scripture to give the deference.

16. For the first of these, I shall propose this consideration, which I had occasion to intimate before, that the Bible being writ for the universal use of the faithful, 'twas as universally disperst amongst them: The Jews had the Law not only in their Synagogues, but in their private houses, and as soon as the Evangelical Books were writ, they were scatter'd into all places where the Christian Faith had obtain'd.   Now when there was such a vast multitude of copies, and those so revered by the possessors, that they thought it the highest pitch of sacrilege to expose them, it must surely be next to impossible, entirely to

U   sup-

suppress that Book. Besides, it could never be attemted but by some eminent violence, as it was by the heathen Persecutors; which (according to the common effect of opposition) serv'd to enhance the Christians value of the Bible; and consequently when the storm was past, to excite their diligence for recruiting the number. So that, unless in after Ages, all the Christians in the world should at once make a voluntary defection, and conspire to eradicate their Religion, the Scriptures could not be utterly extinguish'd.

17. AND that which secures it from total suppression, do's in a great degree do so from corruption and falsification. For whilst so many genuine copies are extant in all parts of the world, to be appeal'd to, it would be a very difficult matter to impose a spurious one; especially if the change were so material as to awaken mens jealousies. And it must be only in a place and age of gross ignorance, that any can be daring enough to attemt it. And if it should happen to succeed in such a particular Church, yet what is that to the universal? And to think to have the forgery admitted there, is (as a learned man saies) like attemting to poison the sea.

18. ON the other side, oral Tradition seems much more liable to hazards, error may there insinuate it self much more insensibly. And tho there be no universal conspiracy

racy to admit it at firſt; yet like a ſmall
eruption of waters, it widens its own paſſage,
till it cauſe an inundation. There is no impreſſion ſo deep, but time and intervening
accidents may wear out of mens minds; e-
ſpecially where the notions are many and
are founded not in nature, but poſitive inſtitution, as a great part of Chriſtian Religion
is. And when we conſider the various tempers of men, 'twill not be ſtrange that ſuc-
ceeding Ages will not alwaies be determin'd
by the Traditions of the former. Some are
pragmatic, and think themſelves fitter to
preſcribe to the belief of their poſterity, than
to follow that of their Anceſtors: ſome have
intereſts and deſigns which will be better ſer-
ved by new Tenets: and ſome are ignorant
and miſtaking, and may unawares corrupt
the doctrine they ſhould barely deliver: and
of this laſt ſort we may gueſs there may be
many, ſince it falls commonly to the mothers lot to imbue children with the firſt ru-
diments.

19. N o w in all theſe caſes how poſſible
is it that primitive Tradition may be either
loſt or adulterated? and conſequently, and
in proportion to that poſſibility, our confidence of it muſt be ſtagger'd. I am ſure according to the common eſtimate in ſeculars
it muſt be ſo. For I appeal to any man whether he be not apter to credit a relation which

U 2   comes

comes from an eie-witnefs than at the third or fourth, much more at the hundredth rebound: (as in this cafe.) And daily experience tells us: that a true and probable ftory by paffing thro many hands, often grows to an improbable lie. This man thinks he could add one becoming circumftance; that man another: and whilft moft men take the liberty to do fo, the relation grows as monftrous as fuch a heap of incoherent phancies can make it.

20. IF to this be faid, that this happens only in trivial fecular matters, but that in the weighty concern of Religion mankind is certainly more ferious and fincere: I anfwer that 'tis very improbable that they are; fince 'tis obvious in the common practice of the world, that the interefts of Religion are poftpon'd to every little wordly concern. And therefore when a temporal advantage requires the bending and warping of Religion, there will never be wanting fom that will attemt it.

21. BESIDES, there is ftill left in human nature fo much of the venom of the Serpents firft temtation, that tho men cannot be as God, yet they love to be prefcribing to him, and to be their own Affeffors as to that worfhip and homage they are to pay him.

22. BUT above all 'tis confiderable that
in

in this cafe Sathan has a more peculiar concern, and can ferve himfelf more by a falfification here than in temporal affairs. For if
he can but corrupt Religion, it ceafes to be
his enemy, and becomes one of his moft
ufeful engins, as fufficiently appear'd in the
rites of the heathen worfhip. We have
therefore no caufe to think this an exemt
cafe; but to prefume it may be influenc'd
by the fame pravity of human nature, which
prevails in others; and confequently are
oblig'd to blefs God that he has not left our
fpiritual concerns to fuch hazards, but has
lodg'd them in a more fecure repofitory, the
written word.

23. But I fore-fee 'twill be objected, that
whilft I thus difparage Tradition, I do vertually invalidate the Scripture it felf, which
comes to us upon its credit. To this I anfwer
firft, that fince God has with-drawn immediate
revelation from the word, Tradition is
the only means to convey to us the firft notice that this Book is the word of God: and
it being the only means he affords, we have
all reafon to depend on his goodnefs, that he
will not fuffer that to be evacuated to us:
and that how liable foever Tradition may be
to err, yet that it fhall not actually err in
this particular.

24. But in the fecond place; This Tradition feems not fo liable to falfification as
others

others: It is fo very fhort and fimple a propo-
fition, fuch and fuch writings are the word
of God, that there is no great room for
Sophiftry or miftake to pervert the fenfe; the
only poffible deception muft be to change the
fubject, and obtrude fuppofititious writings in
room of the true, under the title of the word
of God. But this has already appear'd to be
unpracticable, becaufe of the multitude of
copies which were difperft in the world; by
which fuch an attemt would foon have bin
detected. There appears therefore more reafon as well as more neceffity, to rely upon Tradition in this, than in moft other particulars.

25. NEITHER yet do I fo far decry
oral Tradition in any, as to conclude it impoffible it fhould derive any truth to pofterity:
I only look on it as more cafual; and confequently a lefs fit conveiance of the moft important and neceffary verities than the written Word: In which I conceive my felf jufti-
fi'd by the common fenfe of mankind; who
ufe to commit thofe things to writing, which
they are moft folicitous to derive to pofterity.
Do's any Nation truft their fundamental
Laws only to the memory of the prefent Age,
and take no other courfe to trafmit them
to the future? do's any man purchafe an e-
ftate, and leave no way for his children to
lay claim to it, but the Tradition the prefent
witneffes fhall leave of it? Nay do's any confidering

fidering man ordinarily make any important pact or bargain (tho without relation to pofterity) without putting the Articles in writing? And whence is all this caution but from a univerfal confent that writing is the fureft way of tranfmitting?

26. But we have yet a higher appeal in this matter than to the fuffrage of men: God himfelf feems to have determin'd it; And what his decifion is, 'tis our next bufinefs to inquire.

27. And firft he has given the moft real and comprehenfive atteftation to this way of writing, by having himfelf chofe it. For he is too wife to be miftaken in his eftimate of better and worfe, and too kind to chufe the worft for us: and yet he has chofen to communicate himfelf to the latter Ages of the world by writing; and has fumm'd up all the Eternal concerns of mankind in the facred Scriptures, and left thofe facred Records by which we are to be both inform'd and govern'd; which if oral Tradition would infallibly have done, had bin utterly needlefs: and God fure is not fo prodigal of his fpirit, as to infpire the Authors of Scripture to write that, whofe ufe was fuperfeded by a former more certain expedient.

28. Nay, under the Mofaic oeconomy, when he made ufe of other waies of revealing himfelf, yet to perpetuate the memory even

of

of those Revelations, he chose to have them writen. At the delivery of the Law, God spake then *viva voce*, and with that pomp of dreadfull solemnity, as certainly was apt to make the deepest impressions; yet God fore-saw that thro every succeeding Age that stamp would grow more dim, and in a long revolution might at last be extinct. And therefore how warm soever the Israelites apprehensions then were, he would not trust to them for the perpetuating his Law, but committed it to writing; *Ex.* 31. 18. nay wrote it twice himself.

29. YET farther even the ceremonial Law, tho not intended to be of perpetual obligation, was not yet referr'd to the traditionary way, but was wrote by *Moses*, and deposited with the Priests, *Deut.* 31. 19.   And after-event shew'd this was no needless caution. For when under *Manasses*, Idolatry had prevail'd in *Jerusalem*, it was not by any dormant Tradition, but by the Book of the Law found in the Temple, that *Josiah* was both excited to reform Religion, and instructed how to do it; 2 *Kings* 22. 10.   And had not that or some other copy bin produc'd, they had bin much in the dark as to the particulars of their reformation; which that they had not bin convei'd by Tradition, appears by the sudden startling of the King upon the reading of the Law; which could not have bin, had

had he bin before poffeft with the contents
of it.   In like manner we find in *Nehemiah*,
that the obfervation of the Feaft of Taber-
nacles was recover'd by confulting the Law;
the Tradition whereof was wholly worn out;
or elfe it had fure bin impoffible that it could
for fo long a time have bin intermitted, *Neb.*
1. 18.   And yet mens memories are commonly more retentive of an external vifible rite,
than they are of fpeculative Propofitions, or
moral Precepts.

30. THESE inftances fhew how fallible
an expedient mere oral Tradition is for tranf-
miffion to pofterity.   But admit no fuch inftance could be given, 'tis argument enough
that God has by his own choice of writing,
given the preference to it.   Nor has he barely
chofen it, but has made it the ftandard by
which to meafure all fucceeding pretences.
'Tis the means he prefcribes for diftinguifhing divine from diabolical Infpirations : *To
the Law and to the teftimony : if they fpeak not
according to this Word, there is no light in them,*
Ifai. 8. 20.   And when the Lawyer interroga-
ted our Saviour what he fhould do to inherit
eternal life, he fends him not to ranfack Tradition, or the cabaliftical divinity of the
Rabbins, but refers him to the Law: *What is
written in the Law? how readeft thou?* Luk.
10. 26.   And indeed, throughout the Gofpel,
we ftill find him in his difcourfe appealing to

X   Scri-

Scripture, and afferting its autority: as on the other fide inveighing againft thofe Traditions of the Elders which had evacuated the written Word: *Ye make the Word of God of none effect by your Tradition*, Mat. 15. 6. Which as it abundantly fhews Chrifts adherence to the written word, fo 'tis a pregnant inftance how poffible it is for Tradition to be corrupted, and made the inftrument of impofing mens phancies even in contradiction to Gods commands.

31. AND fince our bleffed Lord has made Scripture the teft whereby to try Traditions, we may furely acquiefce in his decifion, and either embrace or reject Traditions, according as they correfpond to the fupreme rule, the written Word. It muft therefore be a very unwarrantable attemt to fet up Tradition in competition with (much more in contradiction to) that to which Chrift himfelf hath fubjected it.

32. Saint *Paul* reckons it as the principal privilege of the Jewifh Church, that it had the Oracles of God committed to it, *i. e.* that the holy Scriptures were depofited, and put in its cuftody: and in this the Chriftian Church fucceeds it, and is the guardian and confervator of holy Writ. I ask then, had the Jewifh Church by vertue of its being keeper, a power to fuperfede any part of thofe Oracles intrufted to them? if fo, Saint *Paul* was
much

much out in his eftimate, and ought to have
reckon'd that as their higheft privilege.   But
indeed, the very nature of the truft implies
the contrary; and befides, 'tis evident, that
is the very crime Chrift Charges upon the
Jews in the place above cited.   And if the
Jewifh Church had no fuch right, upon what
account can the Chriftian claim any ?   Has
Chrift enlarg'd its Charter ? has he left the
facred Scriptures with her, not to preferve
and practice, but to regulate and reform ? to
fill up its vacancies, and fupply its defects by
her own Traditions? if fo, let the commiffion be produc'd ; but if her office be only
that of guardianfhip and truft, fhe muft neither fubftract from, nor by any fuperaddi-
tions of her own evacuate its meaning and
efficacy: and to do fo, would be the fame
guilt that it would be in a perfon intrufted
with the fundamental Records of a Nation,
to foift in fuch claufes as himfelf pleafes.

33. In fhort, God has in the Scriptures
laid down exact rules for our belief and practice, and has entrufted the Church to convey
them to us: if fhe vary, or any way enervate
them, fhe is falfe to that truft, but cannot by
it oblige us to recede from that rule fhe fhould
deliver, to comply with that fhe obtrudes upon us.   The cafe may be illuftrated by an
eafy refemblance. Suppofe a King have a
foreign principality for which he compofes

a boa body of Laws; annexes to them rewards and penalties, and requires an exact and indispensable conformity to them. These being put in writing, he sends by a select messenger: now suppose this messenger deliver them, yet saies withal, that himself has autority from the King to supersede these Laws at his pleasure; so that their resort must be to his dictates, yet produces no other testimony but his own bare affirmation. Is it possible that any men in their wits should be so stupidly credulous, as to incur the penalty of those Laws upon so improbable an indemnity? And sure it would be no whit less madness in Christians, to violate any precept of God, on an ungrounded supposal of the Churches power to dispense with them.

34. And if the Church universal have not this power, nor indeed ever claim'd it, it must be a strange insolence for any particular Church to pretend to it, as the Church of *Rome* do's; as if we should owe to her Tradition all our Scripture, and all our Faith; insomuch that without the supplies which she affords from the Oracle of her Chair, our Religion were imperfect, and our salvation insecure. Upon which wild dictates I shall take liberty in a distinct Section, farther to animadvert.

SECT.

SECT. VI.

The suffrage of the primitive Christian Church, concerning the propriety and fitness which the Scripture has towards the attainment of its excellent end.

AGAINST what · has bin hitherto said to the advantage of the holy Scripture, there opposes it self (as we have already intimated) the autority of the Church of *Rome*; which allows it to be only an imperfect rule of Faith, saying in the fourth Session of the Council of *Trent*, that *Christian faith and discipline, are contain'd in the Books written, and unwritten Tradition.* And in the fourth rule of the Index put forth by command of the said Council, *the Scripture* is declar'd to be *so far from usefull, that its reading is pernicious, if permitted promiscuously in the vulgar Tongue,* and therefore to be withheld: insomuch that the study of the holy Bible is commonly by persons of the Roman Communion, imputed to Protestants as part of their heresy; they being call'd by them in contemt the Evangelical men, and Scripturarians. And the Bible in the vulgar Tongue of any Nation, is commonly reckon'd among prohibited Books, and as such, publickly burnt

when

when met with by the Inquiſitors: and the perſon who is found with it, or to read therein, is ſubjected to ſevere penalties.

2. For the vindication of the truth of God, and to put to ſhame thoſe unhappy Innovators, who amidſt great pretences to antiquity, and veneration to the Scriptures, prevaricate from both: I think it may not be amiſs to ſhew plainly the mind of the primitive Church herein; and that in as few words as the matter will admit.

3. First I premiſe that *Ireneus* and *Tertullian* having to do with Hereticks, who boaſted themſelves to be emendators of the Apoſtles, and wiſer than they, deſpiſing their autority, rejecting ſeveral parts of the Scripture, and obtruding other writings in their ſtead, have had recourſe unto Tradition, with a ſeeming preference of it unto Scripture. Their adverſaries having no common principle beſides the owning the name of Chriſtians; it was impoſſible to convince them, but by a recourſe to ſuch a medium which they would allow. But theſe Fathers being to ſet down and eſtabliſh their Faith, are moſt expreſs in reſolving it into Scripture: and when they recommend Tradition, ever mean ſuch as is alſo Apoſtolical.

4. Ireneus in the ſecond Book, 37. c. tells us, *that the Scriptures are perfect, as dictated by the word of God and his ſpirit.* And the
same

same Father begins his third Book in this manner, *The disposition of our salvation is no otherwise known by us, than by those by whom the Gospel was brought to us; which indeed they first preach'd, but afterward deliver'd it to us in the Scripture, to be the foundation and pillar of our Faith.   Nor may we imagin, that they began to preach to others, before they themselves had perfect knowledge, as some are bold to say; boasting themselves to be emendators of the Apostles. For after our Lords Resurrection, they were indued with the power of the holy spirit from on high; and having perfect knowledge, went forth to the ends of the earth, preaching the glad tidings of salvation, and celestial praise unto men.   Each and all of whom had the Gospel of God.   So Saint* Matthew *wrote the Gospel to the Hebrews, in their tongue.   Saint* Peter *and   Saint* Paul *preach'd at* Rome, *and there founded a Church:* Mark *the Disciple and interpreter of* Peter, *deliver'd in writing what he had preach'd, and* Luke *the follower of* Paul *set down in his Book the Gospel he had deliver'd.   Afterward Saint* John *at* Ephesus *in* Asia *publish'd his Gospel,* &c.   In his fourth Book, c. 66. he directs all the Hereticks with whom he deals, to *read diligently the Gospel deliver'd by the Apostles, and also read diligently the Prophets,* assuring *they shall there find every action, every doctrine, and every suffering of our Lord declared by them.*

5. THUS

5. THUS *Tertullian* in his Book of Pre-ſcriptions c. 6. *It is not lawfull for us to intro-duce any thing of our own will, nor make any choice upon our arbitrement. We have the Apo-ſtles of our Lord for our Authors, who themſelves took up nothing on their own will or choice; but faithfully imparted to the Nations the diſcipline which they had receiv'd from Chriſt. So that if an Angel from heaven ſhould teach another do-ctrine, he were to be accurſt.* And c. 25. *'Tis madneſs,* ſaies he of the Hereticks, *when they confeſs that the Apoſtles were ignorant of no-thing, nor taught things different; to think that they did not reveal all things to all:* which he enforces in the following Chapter. In his Book againſt *Hermogenes,* c. 23. he diſcourſes thus; *I adore the plenitude of the Scripture, which diſcovers to me the Creator, and what was created. Alſo in the Goſpel I find the Word was the Arbiter and Agent in the Creation. That all things were made of preexiſtent matter I never read.* Let Hermogenes, *and his journey-men ſhew that it is written. If it be not written, let him fear the woe, which belongs to them that add or detract.* And in the 39. ch. of his Preſcript, *We feed our faith, raiſe our hope, and eſtabliſh ur reliance with the ſacred Word.*

6. IN like manner *Hippolytus* in the Ho-mily againſt *Noetus* declares, that *we acknow-ledge only from Scripture that there is one God. And whereas ſecular Philoſophy is not to be had*

*but from the reading of the doctrine of the Philo-
sophers ; so whosoever of us will preserve piety
towards God, he cannot otherwise learn it than
from the holy Scripture.* Accordingly *Origen*
in the fifth Homily on *Leviticus*, saies, that *in
the Scripture every word appertaining to God, is
to be sought and discust ; and the knowledg of all
things is to be receiv'd.*

7. WHAT Saint *Cyprian's* opinion was in
this point, we learn at large from his Epistle
to *Pompey.* For when Tradition was objected to him, he answers; *Whence is this Tradition? is it from the autority of our Lord and
his Gospel ; or comes it from the commands
of the Apostles in their Epistles ? Almighty
God declares that what is written should be
obey'd and practic'd. The Book of the Law,
saies he in* Joshua, *shall not depart from thy
mouth, but thou shalt meditate in it day and
night, that you may observe and keep all that is
written therein. So our Lord sending his Apostles, commands them to baptize all Nations,
and teach them to observe all things that he had
commanded.* Again, *what obstinacy and pre-
sumtion is it to prefer human Tradition to divine command: not considering that Gods wrath
is kindled as often as his Precepts are dissolv'd
and neglected by reason of human Traditions.
Thus God warns and speaks by* Isaiah: *This people honors me with their lips, but their heart is
far from me; but in vain do they worship me,*

Y   *teaching*

teaching for doctrines the commandments of men. *Also the Lord in the Gospel checks and reproves, saying ; you reject the Law of God, that you may establish your Tradition.* Of which Precept the Apostle Saint Paul *being mindful, admonishes and instructs, saying ; If any man teaches otherwise and hearkens not to sound doctrine, and the words of our Lord Jesus Christ, he is proud, knowing nothing : From such we must depart.* And again he adds, *There is a compendious way for religious and sincere minds, both to deposit their errors, and find out the truth. For if we return to the source and original of divine Tradition, human error will cease, and the ground of heavenly mysteries being seen, whatsoever was hid with clouds and darkness, will be manifest by the light of truth. If a pipe that brought plentifull supplies of water, fail on the suddain, do not men look to the fountain, and thence learn the cause of the defect, whether the spring it self be dry; or if running freely, the water is stopt in its passage ; that if by interrupted or broken conveiances, it was hindred to pass, they being repair'd, it may again be brought to the City, with the same plenty as it flows from the spring? And this Gods Priests ought to do at this time, obeying the commands of God, that if truth have swerv'd or fail'd in any particular, we go backward to the source of the Evangelical and Apostolical Tradition, and there found our actings : from whence their order and origination began.*

8. I T

8. IT is true *Bellarmine* reproaches this difcourfe as erroneous; but whatever it might be in the inference which Saint *Cyprian* drew from it, in it felf it was not fo. For Saint *Auftin*,though fufficiently engag'd againft Saint *Cyprian's* conclufion, allows the pofition as moft Orthodox; faying, in the fourth Book of Baptifm, c. 35. *Whereas he admonifhes to go back to the fountain, that is, the Tradition of the Apoftles, and thence bring the ftream down to our times; 'tis moft excellent, and without doubt to be done.*

9. THUS *Eufebius* expreffes himfelf in his fecond Book againft *Sabellius.* *As it is a point of floth, not to feek into thofe things, whereof one may enquire; fo 'tis infolence to be inquifitive in others. But what are thofe things which we ought to enquire into? Even thofe which are to be found in the Scriptures: thofe things which are not there to be found, let us not feek after. For if they ought to be known, the holy Ghoft had not omitted them in the Scripture.*

10. ATHANASIUS in his Tract of the Incarnation, faies, *It is fit for us to adhere to the word of God, and not relinquifh it, thinking by fyllogifms to evade, what is there clearly deliver'd.* Again in his Tract to *Serap.* of the holy Ghoft: *Ask not, faies he, concerning the Trinity, but learn only from the Scriptures. For the inftructions which you will find there, are fufficient.* And in his Oration againft the Gentiles,

Y 2

tiles, declares, *That the Scriptures are sufficient to the manifestation of the truth.*

11. AGREEABLE to these is *Optatus* in his
5. Book against *Parmen.* who reasons thus,
*You say 'tis lawfull to rebaptize, we say 'tis not
lawfull: betwixt your saying and our gain-saying
the peoples minds are amus'd. Let no man believe either you or us. All men are apt to be
contentious. Therefore Judges are to be call'd
in. Christians they cannot be; for they will be
parties; and thereby partial. Therefore a Judge
is to be lookt out from abroad. If a Pagan, he
knows not the mysteries of our Religion. If a
Jew, he is an enemy to our baptism. There is
therefore no earthly Judge; but one is to be sought
from heaven. Yet there is no need of a resort to
heaven, when we have in the Gospel a Testament: and in this case, celestial things may be
compar'd to earthly. So it is as with a Father
who has many children; while he is present he
orders them all, and there is no need of a written
Will: Accordingly Christ when he was present
upon earth, from time to time commanded the
Apostles whatsoever was necessary. But as the
earthly father finding himself to be at the point
of death, and fearing that after his departure
his children should quarrel among themselves, he
calls witnesses, and puts his mind in writing; and
if any difference arise among the brethren, they
go not to their Fathers Sepulcher, but repair to
his Will and Testament; and he who rests in his*
grave,

grave, speakes still in his writing, as if he were alive. *Our Lord who left his Will among us, is now in heaven, therefore let us seek his commands in the Gospel as in his Will.*

12. Thus *Cyril* of *Jeruf.* Cat. 4.   *Nothing, no not the least concernment of the divine and holy Sacraments of our Faith, is to be deliver'd without the holy Scripture: believe not me unless I give you a demonstration of what I say from the Scripture.*

13. Saint *Basil* in his Book of the true Faith saies, *If God be faithful in all his sayings, his words, and works, they remaining for ever, and being done in truth and equity; it must be an evident sign of infidelity and pride, if any one shall reject what is written, and introduce what is not written.*   In which Books he generally declares that he will write nothing but what he receives from the holy Scripture: and that he abhors from taking it elsewhere. In his 29. Homily against the Antitrinit. *Believe,* saies he, *those which are written; seek not those which are not written.*   And in his Eth. reg. 26. *Every word and action ought to be confirm'd by the testimony of the divinely inspir'd Scriptures to the establishment of the Faith of the good, and reproof of the wicked.*

14. Saint *Ambrose* in the first Book of his Offic. saies: *How can we make use of any thing which is not to be found in Scripture?* And in his Institut. of Virgins. *I read he is the first, but*
                                                        read

read not he is the ſecond; let them who ſay he is the ſecond, ſhew it from the reading.

15. G R E G. *Nyſſen* in his Dial. of the ſoul and reſurrect. ſaies, *'Tis undeniable, that truth is there only to be plac'd, where there is the ſeal of Scripture Teſtimony.*

16. S A I N T *Jerom* againſt *Helvidius* declares. *As we deny not that which is written, ſo we refuſe thoſe which are not written.* And in his Comment on the 98. Pſ. *Every thing that we aſſert, we muſt ſhew from the holy Scripture. The word of him that ſpeaks has not that autority as Gods precept.* And on the 87 Pſ. *Whatever is ſaid after the Apoſtles, let it be cut off, nor have afterwards autority. Tho one be holy after the Apoſtles, tho one be eloquent; yet has he not autority.*

17. S A I N T *Auſtin* in his Tract of the unity of the Church, c. 12. *acknowledges that he could not be convinc'd but by the Scriptures of what he was to believe; and adds they are read with ſuch manifeſtation, that he who believes them, muſt confeſs the doctrine to be moſt true.* In the ſecond Book of Chriſtian doctrine, c. 9. he ſaies, that *in the plain places of Scripture are found all thoſe things that concern Faith and Manners.* And in Epiſt. 42. *All things which have bin exhibited heretofore as done to mankind, and what we now ſet and deliver to our poſterity, the Scripture has not paſt them in ſilence, ſo far forth as they concern*
                                                      the

the *search or defence of our Religion.* In his
Tract of the good Widowhood, he faies to
Julian, the person to whom he addreffes,
*What shall I teach you more than that we read in
the Apostle? for the holy Scripture settles the
rule of our doctrine ; that we think not any thing
more than we ought to think ; but to think so-
berly, as God has dealt to every man the measure
of Faith. Therefore my teaching is only to expound the words of this Doctor,* Ep. 157. *Where
any subject is obscure, and passes our comprehension, and the Scripture do's not plainly
afford its help, there human conjecture is presum-
tuous in defining.*

11. THEOPHILUS of *Alex.* in his fecond
Paschal Homily, tells us that *'tis the suggestion
of a diabolical spirit to think that any thing
besides the Scripture has divine autority.* And
in his third he adds, that *the Doctors of the
Church having the Testimony of the Scripture,
lay firm foundation of their doctrine.*

19. CHRYSOSTOM in his third Homily
on the firft of the *Thessal.* afferts, that *from
alone reading or hearing of the Scripture one
may learn all things necessary.* So Hom. 34. on
Acts 15. he declares. *A heathen comes and
faies : I would willingly be a Christian, but I
know not who to join my self to ; for there are
many contentions among you, many seditions and
tumults ; so that I am in doubt what opinion I
should chuse. Each man faies, what I say is*
                                                    true,

true, and I know not whom to believe; each pretends to Scripture which I am ignorant of. 'Tis very well the iſſue is put here: for if the appeal were to reaſon, in this caſe there would be juſt occaſion of being troubled: but when we appeal to the Scriptures, and they are ſimple and certain, you may eaſily your ſelf judge. He that agrees with the Scriptures is a Chriſtian, he that reſiſts them, is far out of the way. *And on Pſ. 95.* If any thing be ſaid without the Scripture, the mind halts between different opinions; ſometimes inclining as to what is probable, anon rejecting as what is frivolous: but when the teſtimony of holy Scripture is produc'd, the mind both of ſpeaker and hearer is confirm'd. *And Hom. 4. on Laʒar.* Tho one ſhould ariſe from the dead, or an Angel come down from heaven, we muſt believe the Scriptures; they being fram'd by the Lord of Angels, and the quick and dead. *And Hom. 13. 2 Cor. 7.* Is it not an abſurd thing that when we deal with men about mony, we will truſt no body, but caſt up the ſum, and make uſe of our counters; but in religious affairs, ſuffer our ſelves to be led aſide by other mens opinions, even then when we have by an exact ſcale and touchſtone, the dictate of the divine Law? Therefore I pray and exhort you, that giving no heed to what this or that man ſaies, you would conſult the holy Scripture, and thence learn the divine riches, and purſue what you have learnt. *And Hom. 58. on Jo. 10. 1.* 'Tis the mark of a thief, that*

that he comes not in by the door, but another way: now by the door the testimony of the Scripture is signified. And Hom. on Gal. 1. 8. *The Apostle saies not, if any man teach a Contrary doctrine let him be accurs'd, or if he subvert the whole Gospel; but if he teach any thing beside the Gospel which you have receiv'd, or vary any little thing, let him be accurs'd.*

20. CYRIL of *Alex.* against *Jul. l.* 7. saies, *The holy Scripture is sufficient to make them who are instructed in it, wise unto salvation, and endued with most ample knowledge.*

21. THEODORET Dial. 1. *I am perswaded only by the holy Scripture.* And Dial. 2. *I am not so bold to affirm any thing, not spoken of in the Scripture.* And again, qu. 45. upon *Genes. We ought not to enquire after what is past over in silence, but acquiesce in what is written.*

22. IT were easy to enlarge this discourse into a Volume; but having taken, as they offer'd themselves, the suffrages of the writers of the four first Centuries, I shall not proceed to those that follow. If the holy Scripture were a perfect rule of Faith and Manners to all Christians heretofore, we may reasonably assure our selves it is so still; and will now guide us into all necessary truth, and consequently make us wise unto salvation, without the aid of oral Tradition, or the new mintage of a living infallible Judge of controversy. And the

Z   impar-

impartial Reader will be enabled to judge whether our appeal to the holy Scripture, in all occaſions of controverſy, and recommendation of it to the ſtudy of every Chriſtian, be that hereſy and innovation which it is ſaid to be.

23. It is, we know, ſeverely imputed to the Scribes and Phariſees by our Savior, that they took from the people *the key of knowledge,* Luke 11. 52. and had *made the word of God of none effect by their Traditions,* Mat. 15. 6. but they never attemted what has bin ſince practiced by their Succeſſors in the Weſtern Church, to take away the Ark of the Teſtament it ſelf, and cut off not only the efficacy, but very poſſeſſion of the word of God by their Traditions. Surely this had bin exceeding criminal from any hand: but that the Biſhops and Governors of the Church and the univerſal and infallible Paſtor of it, who claim the office to interpret the Scriptures, exhort unto, and aſſiſt in the knowledge of them, ſhould be the men who thus rob the people of them, carries with it the higheſt aggravations both of cruelty and breach of truſt. *If any man ſhall take away from the words of the Book of this prophecy* ſaies Saint *John,* Revel. 22. 19. *God ſhall take away his part out of the Book of Life, and out of the holy City, and from the things which*

which are written in this Book. What vengeance therefore awaits thofe, who have taken away not only from one Book, but at once the Books themfelves, even all the Scriptures, the whole word of God?

SECT. VII.

Hiftorical reflexions upon the Events which have happen'd in the Church fince the with-drawing of the holy Scripture.

T WILL in this place be no ufelefs contemplation to obferve, after the Scriptures had bin ravifht from the people in the Church of *Rome*, what pitiful pretenders were admitted to fucceed. And firft becaufe Lay-men were prefum'd to be illiterate, and eafily feducible by thofe writings which were in themfelves difficult, and would be wrefted by the *unlearned to their own deftruction*; pictures were recommended in their ftead, and complemented as the Books of the Laity, which foon emprov'd into a neceffity of their worfhip, and that grofs fuperftition which renders Chriftianity abominated by Turks, and Jews, and Heathens unto this day.

2. I would not be hafty in charging Idolatry upon the Church of *Rome*, or all in her communion; but that their Image-worfhip is a moft fatal fnare, in which vaft numbers of unhappy fouls are taken, no man can doubt who hath with any regard travail'd in Popifh Countries. I my felf, and thoufands of others, whom

whom the late troubles, or other occasions sent abroad, are and have bin witnesses thereof. Charity, 'tis true, believes all things, but it do's not oblige men to disbelieve their eies. 'Twas the out-cry of *Micah* against the Danites, *Jud.* 18. 24. *ye have taken away my Gods which I have made, and the Priest, and are gone away, and what have I more?* but the Laity of the Roman communion may enlarge the complaint, and say; you have taken away the oracles of our God, and set up every where among us graven and molten Images, and Teraphims, and what have we more? and 'twas lately the loud, and I doubt me is still, the unanswerable complaint of the poor *Americans*, that they were deni'd to worship their Pagod once in the year, when they who forbad them, worship'd theirs every day.

3. The Jews before the captivity, notwithstanding the recent memory of the Miracles in Egypt and the Wilderness, and the first conquest of the Land of *Canaan* with those that succeeded under the Judges and Kings of *Israel* and *Juda*; as also the express command of God, and the menaces of Prophets, ever and anon fell to downright Idolatry: but after their return unto this day, have kept themselves from falling into that sin, tho they had no Prophets to instruct them, no miracles or government to encourage or constrain them. The reason of which a very

learned

learned man in his discourse of religious Assemblies takes to be, the reading and teaching of the Law in their Synagogues; which was perform'd with great exactness after the return from the captivity, but was not so perform'd before. And may we not invert the observation, and impute the Image-worship now set up in the Christian Church, to the forbidding the reading of the Scriptures in the Churches, and interdicting the private use, and institution of them?

4. FOR a farther supplement in place of the Scriptures, whose History was thought not edifying enough, the Legends of the Saints were introduc'd; stories so stupid, that one would imagine them design'd as an experiment how far credulity could be impos'd upon; or else fram'd to a worse intent, that Christianity by them might be made ridiculous. Yet these are recommended to use and veneration, while in the mean time the word of God is utterly forbidden, whereby the parties to this unhappy practice (that I may speak in the words of the prophet *Jerem. 2. 13.*) *have committed two evils, they have forsaken the fountain of living waters, and hewed them out cisterns, broken cisterns that can hold no water.*

5. FARTHER yet, the same unreasonable tyranny which permitted not the Laity to understand Almighty God speaking to them in the

the Scripture, hinder'd them from being fuffer'd to understand the Church or themselves speaking to him in their praiers; whilst the whole Roman office is so dispos'd, that in defiance of the Apostles discourse, 1. *Cor.* 14. *he that occupies the room of the unlearned must say amen, to those praiers and praises which he has no comprehension of*: and by his endless repetitions of Paters, Ave's and Credo's, falls into that battology reprov'd by our Savior, *Mat.* 6. 7. And as 'twas said of the woman of *Samaria*, *Jo.* 4. 22. *knows not what he worships.* Yet this unaccountable practice is so much the darling of that Church, that when in *France* about eighteen yeas since, the Roman Miffal was tranflated into the vulgar Tongue, and publifh'd by the direction of feveral of their Bifhops; the Clergy of *France* rofe up in great fury againft the attemt, anathematizing in their circular Epiftles, *all that fold, read, or us'd the faid Book*: and upon complaint unto Pope *Alex.* the 7. he refented the matter fo deeply, as to iffue out his Bull againft it in the following words.

6. WHEREAS *fons of perdition, endeavoring the deftruction of fouls, have tranflated the Roman Miffal into the French Tongue, and fo attemted to throw down and trample upon the majefty of the holy Rites comprehended in Latin words: As we abominate and deteft the novelty, which will deform the beauty of the Church, and produce*
difobe-

disobedience, temerity, boldness, sedition and schism; so we condemn, reprobate and forbid, the said and all other such Translations, and interdict the reading, and keeping, to all and singular the faithful, of whatever sex, degree, order, condition, dignity, honor, or preeminence, &c. under pain of excommunication. And we command the copies to be immediatly burnt, &c. So mortal a sin it seems 'twas thought for the Laity to understand the praiers in which they must communicate.

7. NOR is this all; agreeable to the other attemts upon the holy Scripture, was the bold insolence of making a new authentic Text, in that unknown Tongue in which the offices of praier had bin, and were to be kept disguis'd; which was done by the decree of the Council of *Trent* in the fourth Session. But when the Council had given this Prerogative to the Version which it call'd vulgar, the succeeding Popes began to consider what that Version was; and this work *Pius* the fourth and fifth set upon; but prevented by death fail'd to compleat it, so that the honor of the performance fell to *Sixtus* the fifth, who in the plenitude of his Apostolic power, the Translation being reform'd to his mind, commanded it to be that genuine ancient Edition which the *Trent* Fathers had before made authentic, and under the pain of excommunication requir'd it to be so received: which he do's in this form.

form. *Of our certain knowledge, and the pleni-tude of Apostolic power, we order and declare that the vulgar Edition which has bin receiv'd for authentic by the Council of* Trent, *is without doubt or controversy to be esteem'd this very one, which being amended as well as it is possible, and printed at the Vatican Press, we publish to be read in the whole Christian Republic, and in all Churches of the Christian world. Decreeing that it having bin approv'd by the consent of the holy universal Church, and the holy Fathers, and then by the De-cree of the general Council of* Trent, *and now by the Apostolic autority deliver'd to us by the Lord ; is the true, legitimate, authentic, and undoubted, which is to be received and held in all publick and private Disputations, Lectures, Preach-ings, and Expositions, &c.* But notwithstan-ding this certain knowledge, and plenitude of Apostolic power, soon after came *Clement* the eighth, and again resumes the work of his Predecessor *Sixtus,* discovers great and many errors in it, and puts out one more reform'd, yet confest by himself to be imperfect ; which now stands for the authentic Text, and car-ries the title of the Bible put forth by *Sixtus,* notwithstanding all its alterations. So well do's the Roman Church deserve the honor which she pretends to, of being the *mistress of all Churches* ; and so infallible is the holy Chair in its determinations ; and lastly, so authen-tic a Transcript of the word of God (con-

A a

cerning

cerning which 'tis faid ; *Mat.* 5. 18. *one jot or one title fhall not fail*) is that which fhe eftablifht, and that has receiv'd fo many, and yet according to the confeffion of the infallible Corrector, wants ftill more alterations.

8. DEPENDENT upon this, and as great a mifchief as any of the former, confequent to the with-drawing of the Scripture, I take to be the ftep it made to the overthrow of the ancient and moft ufeful difcipline of the Church in point of Penance, whofe rigors alwaies heretofore preceded the poffibility of having abfolution. Now of this we know a folemn part was the ftate of Audience, when the lapft perfon was receiv'd, after long attendance without doors, proftrations, and lamentations there, within the entrance of the Church ; and was permitted with the Catechumens or Candidates of Baptifm, to hear the readings 'of the Scripture, and ftay till Praier began, but then depart. He was oblig'd to hear the terrors of the Lord, the threats of the divine Law againft fin and finners, to ftand among the unbaptiz'd and heathen multitude, and learn again the elements of that holy Faith from which he had prevaricated; and fo in time be render'd capable of the devotions of the faithful, and afterward of the reception of the Eucharift. But when the Scriptures were thought ufelefs or dangerous to be underftood and heard, it

was

was confequent that the ftate of Audience
fhould be cut off from Penance, and that the
next to it, upon the felf-fame principle fhould
be difmift: and fo the long probation formerly requir'd fhould be fupplanted: and the
compendious way of pardoning firft, and re-
penting afterwards, the endlefs circle of finning and being abfolv'd, and then finning
and being abfolv'd again, fhould prevail upon
the Church. Which ftill obtains, notwithftanding the complaints, and irrefragable demonftrations of learned men even of the Romifh
Communion, who plainly fhew this now receiv'd method, to be an innovation ground-
lefs and unreafonable, and moft pernicious
in its confequents.

9. AND, by the way, we may take notice
that there cannot be a plainer evidence of
the judgement of the Church, concerning the
neceffity of the Scriptures being known, not
only by the learned but mean Chriftian, and
the intereft they have therein, than is the
ancient courfe of Penance, eftablifht by the
practice of all the firft Ages, and almoft
as many Councils, whether general or local,
as have decreed any thing concerning difcipline, with the penitentiary Books and Ca-
nons, which are written for the firft eleven
hundred years in the whole Chriftian world.
For if even the unbaptiz'd Catechumen, and
the lapft finner, notwithftanding their flen-

der

der knowledge in thé myſteries of Faith, or frail pretence to the privilege thereof, had a right to the ſtate of Audience, and was oblig'd to hear the Scripture read; ſurely the meaneſt unobnoxious Laick, was in as advantageous circumſtances, and might not only be truſted with the reading of thoſe ſacred Books, but might claim them as his birth-right.

10. I may juſtly, over and above what has bin hitherto alleg'd, impute to the Governors of the ſame Church, and their withholding from the Laity the holy Scripture, the many dangerous errors, groſs ignorances, and ſcandalous immoralities which have prevail'd among them both. It is no new method of divine vengeance, that there ſhould *be like people, like Prieſt,* Hoſ. 4. 9. *and that the Idle ſhepherd who led his flock into the ditch, ſhould fall therein himſelf,* Mat. 15. 14. And as the Prophet *Zachary* deſcribes it, c. 11. 17. *The ſword ſhall be upon his arm, and upon his right eie: his arm ſhall be clean dried up, and his right eie ſhall be utterly darkned.*

11. But no conſequence can be more obviouſly deducible from that practice, than that men ſhould juſtify the with-holding of the Scripture by leſſening its credit, and depreciating its worth: which has occaſion'd thoſe reproches which by the writers of the Church of *Rome*, of beſt note, have bin caſt

upon

upon it. As that it was *a Nose of wax, a leaden rule, a deaf and useless deputy to God in the office of a judge; of less autority than the Roman Church, and of no more credit than* Esops *Fables, but for the testimony of the said Church; that they contain things apt to raise laughter or indignation, that the Latin Translation in the Complutensian Bible is placed between the Hebrew Text, and the Septuagint Version, as our Savior was at his Crucifixion between two thieves; and that the vulgar Edition is of such autority that the Originals ought to be mended by it, rather than it should be mended from them:* which are the complements of Cardinal *Bellarmin, Hosius, Eckius, Perron, Ximines, Coqueus,* and others of that Communion: words to be answer'd by a Thunderbolt, and fitter for the mouth of a *Celsus* or a *Porphyrie,* than of the pious sons, and zealous Champions of the Church of Christ.

12. Tis to be expected that the Romanists should now wipe their mouths, and plead not guilty; telling us that they permit the Scripture to the Laity in their mother Tongue: And to that purpose the Fathers of *Rhemes* and *Doway* have publisht an English Bible for those of their Communion. I shall therefore give a short and plain account of the whole affair, as really it stands, and then on Gods name let the Romanists make the best of their Apology.

13. THE

13. THE fourth rule of the Index of prohibited Books compos'd upon the command and auspice of the Council of *Trent*, and publish'd by the Autority of *Pius* the fourth, *Sixtus* the fifth, and *Clement* the eighth, runs thus: *Since 'tis manifest by experience, that if the holy Bible be suffer'd promiscuously in the vulgar Tongue, such is the temerity of men, that greater detriment than advantage will thence arise; in this matter let the judgement of the Bishop or Inquisitor be stood to: that with the advice of the Curate or Confessor, they may give leave for the reading of the Bible in the vulgar Tongue, translated by Catholicks, to such as they know will not receive damage, but increase of Faith and Piety thereby. Which faculty they shall have in writing; and whosoever without such faculty shall presume to have or to read the Bible, he shall not till he have deliver'd it up, receive absolution of his sins.* Now (to pass over the iniquity of obliging men to ask leave to do that which God Almighty commands) when tis consider'd how few of the Laity can make means to the Bishop or Inquisitor, or convince them, or the Curate or Confessor, that they are such who will not receive damage, but increase of Faith and Piety by the reading of the Scripture; and also have interest to prevail with them for their favor herein: and after all, can and will be at the charge of taking out the faculty, which is so penally requir'd: 'tis

easy

easy to guess what thin numbers of the Laity are likely, or indeed capable of reaping benefit by this Indulgence pretended to be allowed them.

14. But, besides all this, what shall we say, if the power it self of giving Licences be a mere shew, and really signifies just nothing? In the observation subjoin'd to this fourth rule it is declar'd, that *the Impression and Edition thereof gives no new faculty to Bishops, or Inquisitors, or Superiors of regulars, to grant Licences of buying, reading, or retaining Bibles publisht in a vulgar Tongue; since hitherto by the command and practice of the holy Roman and universal Inquisition, the power of giving such faculties, to read or retain vulgar Bibles, or any parts of Scripture of the Old or New Testament, in any vulgar Tongue; or also summaries or historical compendiums of the said Bibles or Books of Scripture, in whatsoever Tongue they are written, has bin taken away.* And sure if a Lay-man cannot read the Bible without a faculty, and it is not in any ones power to grant it; 'twill evidently follow that he cannot read it: And so the pretence of giving liberty, owns the shame of openly refusing it, but has no other effect or consequence. And if any Romanist among us, or in any other Protestant Country enjoies any liberty herein, 'tis merely by connivance, and owed to a fear left the Votary would be lost, and take the

the Bible where it was without difficulty to be had, if ſtrictneſs ſhould be us'd. And ſhould Popery, which God forbid, become paramount; the Tranſlations of the Scripture into our Mother Tongues, would be no more endur'd here, than they are in *Spain*: and they who have formerly bin wary in communicating the Scriptures, remembring how thereby their errors have bin detected, would upon a revolution effectually provide for the future, and be ſure to keep their people in an Egyptian darkneſs, that might it ſelf be felt, but that allow'd the notices of no other object. They would not be content with that compoſition of the Ammonites, to *thruſt out all the right eies* of thoſe that ſubmitted to them, 1 *Sam.* 11. 2. but would put out both, as the Philiſtins did to *Samſon*, that they might make their miſerable captives for ever *grind in their Mill*, Jud. 16. 21.

15. BUT this heavieſt of judgements will never fall upon the reform'd Churches, till by their vicious practice and contemt of the divine Law, they have deſerted their profeſſion, and made themſelves utterly unworthy of the bleſſings they enjoy, and the light of that Goſpel which with noon-day brightneſs has ſhin'd among them. Upon which account, I ſuppoſe it may not be impertinent in the next place to ſubjoin ſome plain directions, and cautionary advices, concerning the uſe of theſe ſacred Books.

SECT.

S E C T. VIII.

Necessary cautions to be us'd in the reading of the holy Scriptures.

I T is a common observation, that the most generous and sprightly Medicines are the most unsafe, if not appli'd with due care and regimen: And the remark holds as well in spiritual as corporal remedies. The Apostle asserts it upon his own experience, that the doctrine of the Gospel, which was to some *the favor of life unto life, was to others the favor of death,* 2 Cor. 2. 16. And the same effect that the oral Word had then, the written Word may have now; not that either the one or the other have any thing in them that is of it self mortiferous, but becomes so by the ill disposition of the persons who so pervert it. It is therefore well worth our inquiry, what qualifications on our part are necessary to make the Word be to us what it is in it self, *the power of God unto salvation,* Rom. 1. 16. Of these some are previous before our reading, some are concomitant with it; and some are subsequent and follow after it.

2. Of those that go before, sincerity is a most essential requisit: by sincerity, I mean

B b

an

an upright intention, by which we direct our reading to that proper end for which the holy Scriptures were deſign'd: *viz.* the knowing God's will in order to the practicing it. This honeſt ſimplicity of heart is that which Chriſt repreſents by the *good ground*, where alone it was that the ſeed could fructify, *Mat.* 13. 8. And he that brings not this with him, brings only the ſhadow of a Diſciple. The *word of God,* is indeed, *ſharper than a two-edged ſword,* Heb. 4. 12. but what impreſſion can a ſword make on a body of air; which ſtill ſlips from, and eludes its thruſts? And as little can all the practical diſcourſes of Holy Writ make on him, who brings only his ſpeculative faculties with him, and leaves his will and affections behind him; which are the only proper ſubjects for it to work on.

3. To this we may probably impute that ſtrange inefficaciouſneſs we ſee of the Word. Alas, men rarely apply it to the right place: our moſt inveterate diſeaſes lie in our morals; and we ſuffer the Medicine to reach no farther than our intellects. As if he that had an ulcer in his bowels ſhould apply all his balſoms and ſanatives only to his head. 'Tis true, the holy Scriptures are the treaſuries of divine Wiſdom; the Oracles to which we ſhould reſort for ſaving knowledge: but they are alſo the rule and guide of holy Life: and he that covets to know God's will for any purpoſe but to practice

&tice it, is only ftudious to entitle himfelf to the greater number of *ftripes*, Luke 12. 47.

4. N AY farther, he that affects only the bare knowledge, is oft difappointed even of that. The Scripture, like the Pillar of fire and cloud, enlightens the Ifraelites, thofe who fincerely refign themfelves to its guidance; but it darkens and confounds the Egyptians, *Ex.* 14. 20. And 'tis frequently feen, that thofe who read only to become knowing, are toll'd on by their curiofity into the more abftrufe and myfterious parts of Scripture, where they entangle themfelves in inextricable mazes and confufions; and inftead of acquiring a more fuperlative knowledge, loofe thofe eafy and common notions which lie obvious to every plain well meaning Reader. I fear this Age affords too many, and too frequent inftances of this, in men who have loft God in the midft of his Word, and ftudied Scripture till they have renounc'd its Author.

5. A ND fure this infatuation is very juft, and no more than God himfelf has warn'd us of, who *takes the wife in their own craftinefs,* *Job.* 5. 13. but appropriates his *fecrets only to them that fear him,* and has promis'd *to teach the meek his way,* Pfal. 25. 9. 14. And this was the method Chrift obferv'd in his preaching; unveiling thofe truths to his Difciples, which to the Scribes and Pharifees, his inquifitive, yet refractory hearers, he wrapt up in parables,

not

not that he dislik'd their desire of knowledge, but their want of sincerity : which is so fatal a defect as blasts our pursuit, tho of things in themselves never so excellent. This we find exemplifi'd in *Simon Magus*, Acts, 8. who tho he coveted a thing in it self very desirable, the power of conferring the holy Ghost, yet desiring it not only upon undue conditions, but for sinister ends, he not only mist of that, but was (after all his convincement by the Apostles miracles, and the engagement of his Baptism) immerst *in the gall of bitterness*; and at last advanc'd to that height of blasphemy, as to set up himself for a God, so becoming a lasting *memento*, how unsafe it is to prevaricate in holy things.

6. BUT as there is a sincerity of the Will in order to practice, so there is also a sincerity of the understanding in order to belief; and this is also no less requisit to the profitable reading of Scripture. I mean by this, that we come with a preparation of mind, to embrace indifferently whatever God there reveals as the object of our Faith; that we bring our own opinions, not as the clue by which to unfold Scripture, but to be tried and regulated by it. The want of this has bin of very pernicious consequence in matters both of Faith and speculation. Men are commonly prepossest strongly with their own notions, and their errand to Scripture is not to lend them
light

light to judge of them, but aids to back and defend them.

7. OF this there is no Book of controversy that do's not give notorious proof. The Socinian can easily over-look the beginning of Saint *John*, that saies, *The Word was God*, Jo. 1.1. and all those other places which plainly assert the Deity of our Savior; if he can divert to that other more agreeable Text, that *the Father is greater than I.* Among the Romanists, *Peters* being said to be *first among the Apostles*, Mat. 10. 2. and that *on that Rock Christ would build his Church*, Mat. 16. 18. carries away all attention from those other places where Saint *Paul* saies he was not *behind the very chiefest of the Apostles*, 2 Cor. 11. 5. that upon him lay *the care of all the Churches*, 2 Cor. 11. 28. and that the Church was not built upon the *foundation of some one, but all the twelve Apostles*, Revel. 21. 14. So it fares in the business of the Eucharist: *This is my body*, Mat. 26. 26. carries it away clear for Transubstantiation, when our Saviors calling that which he drunk *the fruit of the vine*, Mat. 26. 29. and then Saint *Pauls* naming the Elements in the Lords Supper several times over, Bread and Wine; *The Bread that we break, is it not the Communion of the Body of Christ: The Cup that we bless, is it not the Communion, &c.* 1 Cor. 10. 16. And again, *He that eats this Bread, and drinks this Cup unworthily, &c.* 1 Cor. 11. 29.

29. can make no appearance of an Argument.

8. THUS men once engag'd, ranfack for Texts that carry fome correfpondency to the opinions they have imbibed, and thofe how do they rack and fcrue to bring to a perfect conformity: and improve every little probability in a demonftration? On the other fide the contrary Texts they look on as enemies, and confider them no farther than to provide fences and guards againft them: So they bring Texts not into the fcales to weigh, but into the field to skirmifh, as Partizans and Auxiliaries of fuch or fuch opinions.

9. BY this force of prepoffeffion it is, that that facred rule, which is the meafure and ftandard of all rectitude, is it felf bow'd and diftorted to countenance and abet the moft contrary tenets: and like a variable picture, reprefents differing fhapes according to the light in which you view it. And fure we cannot do it a worfe office than to reprefent it thus diffonant to it felf. Yet thus it muft ftill be till men come unbiaft to the reading of it. And certainly there is all the reafon in the world they fhould do fo: the ultimate *end of our faith is but the falvation of our fouls,* 1 Pet. 1. 9. and we may be fure the Scripture can beft direct us what Faith it is which will lead us to that end.

10. WHY

10. WHY should we not then have the same indifference which a traveller hath, whether his way lie on this hand or that : so as it be the direct road to his journies end ? For although it be infinitely material that I embrace right principles, yet 'tis not so that this should be right rather than the other : and our wishes that it should be so, proceed only from our prepossessions and fondness of our own conceptions, than which nothing is more apt to intercept the clear view of truth. It therefore nearly concerns us to deposit them, and to give up our selves without reserve to the guidance of Gods Word, and give it equal credit when it thwarts, as when it complies with our own notions.

11. WITHOUT this, tho we may call Scripture the rule of Faith, and judge of controversies; yet 'tis manifest we make it not so, but reserve still the last appeal to our own prejudicate phancies : and then no wonder, though we fall under the same occecation which our Savior upbraids to the Jews, *that seeing, we see not, neither do we understand,* Mat. 13.14. For he that will not be sav'd Gods way, will hardly be so by his own. He that resolves not impartially to embrace all the Scriptures dictates, comes to them as unsincerely, as the remnant of the Jews did to *Jeremiah* to inquire of the Lord for them, which he no sooner had done, but they protest against his mes-

fage, *Jer* 42. 20. and may expect as fatal an
event.

12. BUT there are a fet of men who deal
yet more unfincerely with the Word; that
read it infidioufly, on purpofe to collect matter of objection and cavil; that with a malicious diligence compare Texts in hope to
find contradictions; and read attentively, but
to no other end than to remark incoherences
and defects in the ftile: which when they
think they have ftarted, they have their defign; and never will ufe a quarter of the
fame diligence in confidering how they may
be folv'd, or confulting with thofe who may
affift them in it.   For I think I may appeal to
the generality of thofe who have rais'd the
loudeft clamors againft the Scripture, whether they have endeavor'd to render themfelves competent judges of it by inquiring into the Originals, or informing themfelves of
thofe local Cuftoms, peculiar Idioms, and many other circumftances, by which obfcure
Texts are to be clear'd.   And tho I do not affirm it neceffary to falvation that every man
fhould do this; yet I may affirm it neceffary
to him that will pretend to judge of the Bible: and he that without this condemns it, do's
it as manifeft injury, as a judge that fhould
pafs fentence only upon the Indictment,
without hearing the defence.

13. AND certainly there cannot be any
thing

thing more unmanly and difingenuous, than for men to inveigh and condemn before they inquire and examine. Yet this is the thing upon which fo many value themfelves, affuming to be men of reafon, for that for which the Scripture pronounces them brute Beafts, viz. *the fpeaking evil of thofe things they under-ftand not,* 2 Pet. 2. 12. Would men ufe due diligence, no doubt many of thofe feeming contradictions would be reconcil'd, and the obfcurities clear'd: and if any fhould after all remain, they might find twenty things fitter to charge it on, than want of verity or difcourfe in the infpir'd writers.

14. ALAS what human writing is there of near that Antiquity, wherein there are not many paffages unintelligible? And indeed, unlefs modern times knew all thofe national cuftoms, obfolete Laws, particular Rites and Ceremonies, Phrafes and proverbial Sayings, to which fuch ancient Books refer, 'tis impoffible but fome paffages muft ftill remain obfcure. Yet in thefe we ordinarily have fo much candor, as to impute their unintelligiblenefs to our own ignorance of thofe things which fhould clear them, the improprieties of ftile to the variation that times make in dialects, or to the errors of Scribes, and do not prefently exclaim againft the Authors as falfe or impertinent, or difcard the whole Book for fome fuch paffages.

C c

15. AND

15. And sure what allowances we make to other Books, may with more reason be made to the Bible; which having bin writ so many Ages since, past thro infinite variety of hands, and (which is above all) having bin the object of the Devils, and wicked mens malice, lies under greater disadvantages than any human composure: And doubtless men would be as equitable to that as they are to others, were it not that they more wish to have that false or irrational than any other Book. The plain parts of it, the precepts and threatnings speak clearer than they desire, gall and fret them; and therefore they will revenge themselves upon the obscurer: and seem angry that there are some things they understand not, when indeed their real displeasure is at those they do.

16. A second qualification preparatory to reading the Scripture is reverence. When we take the Bible in our hands, we should do it with other sentiments and apprehensions than when we take a common Book; considering that it is the word of God, the instrument of our salvation; or upon our abuse of it, a promoter of our ruin.

17. And sure this, if duly apprehended, cannot but strike us with a reverential awe, make us to say with *Jacob*, Gen. 28. 14. *surely God is in this place*; controul all trifling phancies, and make us read, not for custom or divertise-

vertifement, but with thofe folemn and holy intentions which become the dignity of its Author. Accordingly we find holy men have in all Ages bin affected with it; and fome to the inward reverence of the mind, have join'd the outward of the body alfo, and never read it but upon their knees: an example that may both inftruct and reproach our profanefs; who commonly read by chance, and at a venture: If a Bible happen in our way, we take it up as we would do a Romance, or Play-book; only herein we differ, that we difmifs it much fooner, and retain lefs of its impreffions.

18. It was a Law of *Numa*, that no man fhould meddle with divine things, or worfhip the Gods, in paffing or by accident, but make it a fet and folemn bufinefs. And every one knows with how great ceremony and folemnity the heathen Oracles were confulted. How great a fhame is it then for Chriftians to defalk that reverence from the true God, which heathens allow'd their falfe ones?

19. Now this proceeds fometimes from the want of that habitual reverence we fhould alwaies have to it as Gods word, and fometimes from want of actual exciting it, when we go to read: for if the habit lie only dormant in us, and be not awak'd by actual confideration, it avails us as little in our reading, as the habitual ftrength of a man do's towards labor

bor

bor, when he will not exert it for that end.

20. WE ought therefore, as to make it our deliberate choice to read Gods word; so when we do it, to stir up our selves to those solemn apprehensions of its dignity and autority, as may render us malleable, and apt to receive its impressions; for where there is no reverence, 'tis not to be expected there should be any genuine or lasting obedience.

21. SAINT *Austin* in his Tract to *Honoratus*, of the advantage of believing, makes the first requisite to the knowledge of the Scriptures to be the love of them. *Believe me, saies he, every thing in the Scripture is sublime and divine, its truth and doctrine are most accommodate to the refreshment, and building up of our minds: and in all respects so order'd, that every one may draw thence what is sufficient for him; provided he approach it with devotion, piety, and religion. The proof of this may require much reasoning and discourse. But this I am first to perswade, that you do not hate the Authors, and then that you love them. Had we an ill opinion of* Virgil, *nay, if upon the account of the reputation he has gain'd with our Predecessors, we did not greatly love, before we understood him; we should never patiently go through all the difficult questions Grammarians raise about him. Many employ themselves in commenting upon him; we esteem him most, whose exposition most commends the Book, and shews that the*

the Author, not only was free from error, but did excellently well where he is not understood. And if such an account happen not to be given, we impute it rather to the Interpreter than the Poet.

22. THUS the good Father; whose words I have transcrib'd at large, as being remarkable to the present purpose; he also shews that the mind of no Author is to be learnt from one averse to his doctrine: as that 'tis vain to enquire of *Aristotles* Books from one of a different Sect: Or of *Archimedes* from *Epicurus*: the discourse will be as displeasing as the speaker; and that shall be esteem'd absurd, which comes from one that is envi'd or despis'd.

23. A third preparative to our reading should be praier. The Scripture as it was dictated at first by the holy Spirit, so must still owe its effects and influence to its cooperation. *The things of God,* the Apostle tells us, *are spiritually discern'd,* 1 Cor. 2. 14. And though the natural man may well enough apprehend the letter, and grammatical sense of the Word; yet its power and energy, that insinuative perswasive force whereby it works on hearts, is peculiar to the spirit; and therefore without his aids, the Scripture whilst it lies open before our eies, may still be *as a Book that is seal'd,* Esai. 29. 11. be as ineffective as if the characters were illegible.

24. BE-

24. BESIDES our Savior tells us the devil is still busy *to steal away the feed as soon as it is sown*, Mat. 13. 19. And unless we have some better guard than our own vigilance, he is sure enough to prosper in his attemt. Let it therefore be our care to invoke the divine Aid; and when ever we take the Bible into our hands, to dart up at least a hearty ejaculation, that we may find its effects in our hearts. Let us say with holy *David, open thou mine eies O Lord, that I may fee the wondrous things of thy Law. Blessed art thou O Lord, O teach me thy statutes*, Pf. 119. Nay indeed 'twill be fit matter of a daily solemn devotion, as our Church has made it an annual in the Collect on the second Sunday in Advent: a praier so apt and fully expressive of what we should desire in this particular, that if we transcribe not only the example, but the very words, I know not how we can form that part of our devotion more advantageously.

25. IN the second place we are to consider what is requir'd of us at the time of reading the Scripture; which consists principally in two things. The first of these is attention, which is so indispensably requisite, that without it all Books are alike, and all equally insignificant: for he that adverts not to the sense of what he reads, the wisest discourses signify no more to him, than the most exquisite musick do's to a man perfectly deaf. The letters and
sylla-

syllables of the Bible are no more sacred than those of another Book; 'tis the sense and meaning only that is divinely inspir'd: and he that considers only the former, may as well entertain himself with a spelling-book.

26. We must therefore keep our minds fixt and attent to what we read: 'tis a folly and lightness not to do so in human Authors; but 'tis a sin and danger not to do so in this divine Book. We know there can scarce be a greater instance of contemt and disvalue, than to hear a man speak, and not at all mind what he saies: yet this vilest affront do all those put upon God, who hear or read his Word, and give it no attention. Yet I fear the practice is not more impious than it is frequent: for there are many that read the Bible, who if at the end of each Chapter they should be call'd to account, I doubt they could produce very slender collections: and truly 'tis a sad consideration, that that sacred Book is read most attentively by those, who read it as some *preach the Gospel,* Phil. 1. 15. *out of envy and strife.* How curiously do men inspect, nay ransack and embowel a Text to find a pretence for cavil and objection, whilst men who profess to look there for life and salvation, read with such a retchless heedlesness, as if it could tell them nothing they were concern'd in: and to such 'tis no wonder if their reading bring no advantage. God is

not

not in this sense *found of those that seek him not*, Esai. 65. 1. 'tis Satans part to serve himself of the bare words and characters of holy Writ, for charms and amulets: the vertue God has put there consists in the sense and meaning, and can never be drawn out by drousy inadverting Readers.

27. THIS unattentiveness fore-stalls all possibility of good. How shall that convince the understanding, or perswade the affections, which do's not so much as enter the imagination. So that in this case the seed seems more cast away than in any of those instances the parable gives, *Mat.* 13. In those it still fell upon the soil, but in this it never reaches that; but is scatter'd and dissipated, as with a mighty wind, by those thoughts which have prepossess'd the mind. Let no man therefore take this sacred Book into his hand, till he have turn'd out all distracting phansies, and have his faculties free and vacant for those better objects which will there present themselves. And when he has so dispos'd himself for attention, then let him contrive to improve that attention to the best advantage.

28. To which purpose it may be very conducive to put it into some order and method. As for instance, when he reads the doctrinal part of Scripture, let him first and principally advert to those plain Texts which contain
                                    the

the neceſſary points of Faith: that he may not owe his Creed only to his education, the inſtitution of his Parents or Tutors; but may know the true foundation on which it is bottom'd, *viz.* the word of God, and may thence be able to juſtify his Faith: and as Saint *Peter exhorts*, be ready to give an anſwer to *every man that asks him a reaſon of the hope that is in him*, 1 Pet. 3. 15. For want of this it is, that Religion ſits ſo looſe upon men, that every wind of doctrine blows them into diſtinct and various forms; till at laſt their Chriſtianity it ſelf vapors away and diſappears.

29. But let men be careful thus to ſecure the foundation, and then 'twill be commendable in them (who are capable of it) to aſpire to higher degrees of ſpeculation: yet even in theſe it will be their ſafeſt courſe chiefly to purſue ſuch as have the moſt immediate influence on practice, and be more induſtrious to make obſervations of that ſort, than curious and critical remarks, or bold conjectures upon thoſe myſteries on which God has ſpread a veil.

30. But beſides a mans own particular collections, it will be prudence in him to advantage himſelf of thoſe of others, and to conſult the learnedſt and beſt expoſitors; and that not only upon a preſent emergency, when he is to diſpute a point, (as moſt do) but

D d

but in the constant course of his reading, wherein he will most sedately, and dispassionately judge of the notions they offer.

31. As to the choice of the portions of Scripture to be read in course, though I shall not condemn that of reading the whole Bible in order, yet 'tis apparent that some parts of it (as that of the Levitical Law) are not so aptly accommodated to our present state, as others are; and consequently not so edificatory to us: and therefore I cannot see why any man should oblige himself to an equal frequency in reading them. And to this our Church seems to give her suffrage, by excluding such out of her publick Lessons. And if we govern our private reading by her measure it will well express our deference to her judgement; who has selected some parts of Scripture, not that she would keep her children in ignorance of any, but because they tend most immediately to practice.

32. Neither will the daily reading the Scripture in the rubricks order, hinder any man from acquainting himself with the rest. For he may take in the other parts as supernumeraries to his constant task, and read them as his leisure and inclination shall prompt. So that all the hurt that can accrue to him by this method, is the being invited to read sometimes extraordinary proportions.

33. If it be objected, that to those who
daily

daily hear the Church Service, 'twill be a kind of tautology, first to read those Lessons in private, which soon after they shall hear read publickly; I answer that whatever men may please to call it, 'twill really be an advantage: For he that shall read a chapter by himself with due consideration, and consulting of good Paraphrasts, will have div'd so far into the sense of it, that he will much better comprehend it when he hears it read: as on the other side, the hearing it read so immediatly after will serve to confirm and rivet the sense in his mind. The one is as the conning, the other the repeating the Lesson; which every School-boy can tell us is best done at the nearest distance to each other. But I shall not contend for this, or any particular method: let the Scriptures be read in proportion to every mans leisure and capacity, and read with attention; and we need not be scrupulous about circumstances when the main duty is secur'd.

34. BUT as in the doctrinal, so in the preceptive part, there is a caution to be us'd in our attention. For we are to distinguish between those temporary precepts that were adapted to particular times and occasions, and such as are of perpetual obligation. He that do's not this, may bring himself under the Jewish Law, or believe a necessity of selling all and giving it to the poor because 'twas

D d 2   Christs

Chrifts command to the rich man; *Mat.* 19. or incur other confiderable mifchiefs.

35. THUS frequently commands are put in comprehenfive indefinite words, but concern only the generality to whom the Law is written; and not thofe who are intrufted with the vindication of their contemt. Accordingly 'tis faid, *thou fhalt not kill,* Mark. 10. 19. which concerns the private perfon; but extends not to the Magiftrate in the execution of his office, who *is a revenger* appointed by God, *and bears not the fword in vain,* Rom. 13. 4. So the injunction not *to fwear at all,* Mat. 5. 34. refers to the common tranfactions of life; but not thofe folemn occafions where an oath is to give glory to God, *and is the end of all ftrife,* Heb. 6. 16. Yet thefe miftakes at this day prevail with Anabaptifts and Quakers, and bottom their denial of the Magiftrates power to protect his Subjects by war; and to determin differences in Peace, by the oath of witneffes in judicial proceedings.

36. THERE is another diftinction we are to attend to; and that is between abfolute and primary commands, and fecundary ones: the former we are to fet a fpecial remark upon, as thofe upon whofe obfervance or violation our eternal life or death infeparably depends. And therefore our firft and moft folicitous care muft be concerning them. I mention this
not

not to divert any from aspiring to the highest
degrees of perfection : but to reprove that
preposterous course many take, who lay
the greatest weight upon those things on
which God laies the least; and have more
zeal for oblique intimations, than for express downright commands; nay think by
the one to commute for the contemt of the
other. For example, fasting is recommended to us in Scripture, but in a far lower key
than moral duties: rather as an expedient
and help to vertue, than as properly a vertue it self. And yet we may see men scrupulous in that, who startle not at injustice, and
oppression (that clamorous sin that cries to
heaven) who pretend to mortify their appetites by denying it its proper food or being
luxurious in one sort of it; and yet glut their
avarice, eat up the poor, *and devour widows
houses*, Mat. 23.

37. To such as these twould be good advice to fix their attention on the absolute
commands, to study moral honesty and the
essentials of Christianity; to make a good
progress there, and do what God indispensably requires: and then it may be seasonable
to think of voluntary oblations: but till then
they are so far from homage, that they are
the most reproachful flattery; an attemt to
bribe God against himself; and a sacrilege,
like that of *Dionysius*, who took away *Apollo's*

'*s* golden robe, and gave him a stuff one.

38. THE second thing requisit in our reading is application: this is the proper end of our attention:. and without this we may be very busy to very little purpose. The most laborious attention without it, puts us but in the condition of those poor slaves that labor in the mines; who with infinite toil dig that ore of which they shall never partake. If therefore we will appropriate that rich treasure, we must apply, and so make it our own.

39. LET us then at every period of holy Writ, reflect and look on our selves as the persons spoke to. When we find *Philip* giving baptism to the Eunuch upon this condition, that he *believe with all his heart*, Act. 8. let us consider that unless we do so, our baptism (like a thing surreptitiously obtain'd) conveys no title to us; will avail us nothing.

40. WHEN we read our Saviours denunciation to the Jews, *except ye repent, ye shall all likewise perish*; Luke 13. 5. we are to look on it as if addrest immediatly to our selves; and conclude as great a necessity of our repentance. In those black catalogues of crimes which the Apostle mentions, 1 *Cor.* 6. 10. and *Gal.* 5. 19, 20, 22. as excluding from the Kingdom of heaven, we are to behold our own guilts arraign'd, and to resolve that the same crimes will as certainly shut heaven gates against us, as those to whom those Epistles were

imme-

immediatly directed. In all the precepts of good life, and Chriftian vertue, we are to think our felves as nearly and particularly concern'd, as if we had bin Chrifts Auditors on the mount. So proportionably in all the threats and promifes we are either to tremble or hope, according as we find our felves adhere to thofe fins or vertues to which they are affixt.

41. This clofe application would render what we read operative and effective, which without it will be ufelefs and infignificant. We may fee an inftance of it in *David*; who was not at all convinc'd of his own guilt by *Nathans* parable (tho the moft appofite that was imaginable) till he roundly apply'd it, faying, *thou art the man.* 2 Sam. 12. And unlefs we treat our felves at the fame rate, the Scripture may fill our heads with high notions, nay with many fpeculative truths, which yet amounts to no more than the Devils theology, *Ja.* 2. 19. and will as little advantage us.

42. It now remains that we fpeak of what we are to do after our reading; which may be fumm'd up in two words: Recollect and practice. Our memories are very frail as to things of this nature. And therefore we ought to imprefs them as deep as we can, by reflecting on what we have read. It is an obfervation out of the Levitical Law, that
thofe

thofe beafts only were clean, and fit for fa-
crifice, *that chew'd the cud*, Lev. 11. 4. And tho
the ceremony were Jewifh, the moral is Chriftian, and admonifhes us how we fhould re-
volve and ruminate on fpiritual inftructions.
Without this what we hear or read flips in-
fenfibly from us, and like letters writ in chalk,
is wip't out by the next fucceeding thought:
but recollection engraves and indents the
characters in the mind. And he that would
duly ufe it, would find other manner of impreffions; more affective and more lafting
than bare reading will leave.

43. W E find it thus in all Sciences: he
that only reads over the rules, and laies afide
the thoughts of them together with his Book,
will make but a flow advance; whilft he that
plods and ftudies upon them, repeats and rein-
forces them upon his mind, foon arives to an
eminency. By this it was that *David* attain'd
to that perfection in Gods Law as to out-ftrip
his teachers, *and underftand more than the Anci-*
ents, Pfal. 119. 99, 100. becaufe it was his *medi-*
tation as himfelf tells us, *ver.* 97. 99.

44. L E T us therefore purfue the fame method; and when we have read a portion of
Scripture, let us recollect what obfervable
things we have there met with: what exhortations to vertue, or determents from vice;
what promifes to obedience, or menaces for
the contrary; what examples of Gods vengeance

geance againſt ſuch or ſuch ſins, or what in-
ſtances of his bleſſing upon duties. If we do
this daily, we cannot but amaſs together a
great ſtock of Scripture documents, which
will be ready for us to produce upon every
occaſion. Satan can aſſault us no where, but
we ſhall be provided of a guard, a *Scriptum
eſt;* which we ſee was the ſole armor the ca-
ptain of our Salvation us'd in his encounter
with him, *Mat.* 4. *ver.* 4. 7. and 10. and will
be as ſucceſsful to us, if we will duly ma-
nage it.

45. The laſt thing requir'd as conſequent
to our reading, is practice. This is the ultimate end, to which all the fore-going qualifications are directed. And if we fail here,
the moſt aſſiduous diligence in all the former
will be but loſt labor. Let us mean never ſo
well, attend never ſo cloſe, recollect never ſo
exactly; if after all we do not practice, all the
reſt will ſerve but to enhance our guilt. Chriſtianity is an active Science, and the Bible was
given us not merely for a theme of ſpeculation,
but for a rule of life.

46. And alas, what will it avail us that our
opinions are right, if our manners be crook-
ed? When the Scripture has ſhew'd us what
God requires of us, nay, has evinc'd to us the
reaſonableneſs of the injunctions, the great a-
greeableneſs which they have to the excellency of our nature: and has backt this with

E e the

the assurance that *in keeping of them there shall be a great reward,* Pf. 19. 11. if in the midst of such importunate invitations to life we will choose death; we are indeed *worthy,* as the wise man speaks, *to take part with it,* Wif. 1. 16. our crimes are hereby increas'd to a monstrous bulk, and also depriv'd of that veil and shelter which darkness and ignorance would have given them. And a vicious Christian may have cause at the last day to wish that he had studied the Alcoran rather than the Bible. His sensualities might then have pleaded, that they were but the anticipating his Paradise, taking up that before hand, which his Religion propos'd to him as his *summum bonum,* his final and highest aim. But with what confusion must a Christian then appear, whose institution obliges him to mortify the flesh: and yet has made it the business of his life, not only to satisfy, but even to enrage, and enflame its appetites? that has set up a counter-discipline to that of the Gospel he professes; and when that requires austerities and self-denials, to reduce corrupt nature to a tameness and subjection, has not only pull'd off the bridle, but us'd the spur; contriv'd Arts to debauch even corruption it self; and has forc'd his relucting nature upon studied and artificial leudness? Such men may be thought to have read the Scripture with no other design but to be sure to

run

run counter to it; that by informing themselves of Gods will, they may know the more exactly how to affront and contradict it.

47. Nay, so it is, too many unto malice add contempt; are not content only sullenly to resist its Precepts, but despise and revile them also, arraign the wisdom of God, and pronounce the divine Laws to be weak and impertinent; lay their Scenes of ridiculous mirth in the Bible; rally in the sacred Dialect, and play the Buffoons with the most serious thing in the world. An impious licentiousness which is now grown to that height, that it is one of the wonders of Gods long-suffering that there are not as many eminent instances of the vengeance, as there are of the guilt. I have formerly complain'd of it, and must still crave leave to do so. It is indeed so spreading an infection, that we can never be sufficiently arm'd against it. Some degrees of it have tainted many who have not utterly renounc'd their reverence for the Bible: there being those who in their solemn moods own it as Gods word, and profess they must finally stand or fall by its verdict; who yet in their jocular humors make light and irreverent applications of its phrases and sentences, furnish out their little jests in its attire, and use it as if they thought it good for nothing else.

48. And certainly this abuse in men that own the Bible, is infinitly more monstrous

E e 2 than

than in thoſe who defy it : the latter look on it as a common thing, and uſe it as ſuch : but for thoſe who confeſs it ſacred, thus to proſtitute it, is a flat contradiction as much againſt the rules of Diſcourſe as Religion : 'tis to offer the ſame abuſe to Chriſt in his Word, which the rude ſoldiers did to his perſon ; to bow the knee before it, and yet expoſe it as an object of ſcorn and laughter. But ſure there cannot be two things more inconſiſtent, than the avowing it to be dictated by God in order to the moſt important concern of man, and yet debaſe it to the vileſt purpoſes ; make it the drudge and hackney to our ſportful humors, and bring it out as the Philiſtins did *Samſon,* only to make us merry, *Jud.* 16. 25.

49. I N D E E D one would wonder how that ſhould become a proper inſtrument for that purpoſe, that thoſe doctrines of righteouſneſs, temperance and judgment to come (every where ſcatter'd thro that Book) which ſet heathen *Felix* a trembling, ſhould ſet Chriſtians a laughing : and yet ſhould men cite the ſame things and phraſes out of another Author, there would be no jeſt in it. It ſeems therefore that the ſpirit and eſſence of this ſort of wit lies in the profaneſs. How abſurd is it then for men that do not utterly abjure Religion, to affect this impious ſort of raillery, which has nothing but daring wickedneſs

kednefs to recommend it? for certainly, of all the waies of difcourfe that ever pretended to wit, this has the leaft claim to it.

50. WHAT ftrength of reafon, or height of phancy is there in repeating of phrafes and fragments of Books, when what they would fay, they might much more properly exprefs in their own words? In any other inftance but this of the Bible, it would pafs rather for a defect than an excefs of wit. But that which I fuppofe renders it fo taking, is, that it is the cheapeft expedient for men to arrive to that reputation. Men that cannot go to the coft of any thing that is truly ingenious, can by this means immediatly commence wits; if they can but charge their memories with half a dozen Texts, they need no other furniture for the trade: thefe mangled and tranfpofed, will be ready at all turns, and render them applauded by thofe who have no other meafure of wit, but its oppofition to Piety. But would God, men would look a little before them; and confider what the final reckoning will be for fuch divertifements; and if the whole world be an unequal exchange for a foul, what a miferable Merchant is he that barters his for a bald infipid jeft? fuch as a fober man would avoid were there no fin in it.

51. I know men are apt to flatter themfelves, that thefe lighter frolicks will pafs for

nothing,

nothing, so long as they do not seriously and maliciously oppose Gods word: but I fear they will find God in earnest, tho they be in jest. He that has *magnified his Word above all things*, Psal. 138. 2. cannot brook that we should make it vile and cheap, play and dally with it. And if it were a capital crime to convert any of the perfume of the Sanctuary to common use, *Ex.* 30. 32. can we think God can be pleas'd to see his more sacred Word, the theme of our giddy mirth, and have his own words ecchoed to him in profane drollery?

52. B u t besides 'tis to be consider'd that this wanton liberty is a step to the more solemn and deliberate contemt of Gods word: custom do's strangely prescribe to us, and he that a while has us'd any thing irreverently, will at last bring his practice into argument, and conclude that there is no reverence due to it. God knows we are naturally too apt to slight and easy apprehensions of sacred things; and had need to use all Arts and Instruments to impress an awe upon our minds.

53. I t will sure then be very unsafe for us to trifle with them, and by so undue a familiarity draw on that contemt which we should make it our care to avoid. The wise man saies, *he that contemns small things, shall fall by little and little*, Eccl. 19. 1. And tho no degree of irreverence towards God or his
Word,

Word, can be call'd a small thing absolutely consider'd, yet comparatively with the more exorbitant degrees it may: and yet that smaller is the seed and parent of the greatest. It is so in all sins, the kingdom of Satan, like that of God, may be compar'd to *a grain of mustard seed*, Mat. 13. 31. which tho little in it self, is mighty in its increase.

54. No man ever yet began at the top of villany, but the advance is still gradual from one degree to another; each commission smoothing and glibbing the way to the next. He that accustoms in his ordinary discourse, to use the sacred Name of God with as little sentiment and reverence, as he do's that of his neighbor or servant; that makes it his common by-word, and cries Lord and God upon every the highest occasion of exclamation to wonder, this man has a very short step to the using it in oaths, and upon all frivolous occasions; and he that swears vainly, is at no great distance from swearing falsely. It is the same in this instance of the Scriptures: He that indulges his wit to rally with them, will soon come to think them such tame things that he may down-right scorn them: And when he is arriv'd to that, then he must pick quarrels to justify it, till at last he arrive even to the height of enmity.

55. Let every man therefore take heed of setting so much as one step in this fatal circle;

circle; guard himfelf againſt the firſt inſinuation of this guilt: and when a jeſt offers it felf as a temtation, let him balance that with a fober thought, and confider whether the jeſt can quit the coſt of the profanation. Let him poſſeſs his mind with an habitual awe, take up the Bible with folemner thoughts, and other kind of apprehenſions than any human Author: and if he habituate himſelf to this reverence, every clauſe and phraſe of it that occurs to his mind, will be apter to excite him to devout ejaculations than vain laughter.

56. I T is reported of our excellent Prince, King *Edward* the fixth; that when in his Council Chamber, a Paper that was call'd for, happen'd to lie out of reach, and the Perſon concern'd to produce it, took a Bible that lay by, and ſtanding upon it reacht down the Paper: the King obferving what was done, ran himſelf to the place, and taking the Bible in his hands, kiſſed it, and laid it up again. Of this it were a very defirable moral, that Princes, and all perſons in autority, would take care not to permit any to raiſe themſelves by either a hypocritical or profane trampling upon holy things. But befides that, a more general application offers its felf; that all men of what condition foever, ſhould both themſelves abſtain from every action that has the appearance of a
con-

contemt of the holy Scripture; and also when they obferve it in others, difcountenance the infolence : and by their words and actions give Teftimony of the veneration which they have for that holy Book, they fee others fo wretchedly defpife.

57. BUT above all, let him who reads the Scripture, ferioufly fet himfelf to the practice of it, and daily examine how he proceeds in it : he that diligently do's this, will not be much at leifure to fport with it : he will fcarce meet with a Text which will not give him caufe of reflection, and provide him work within his own breft : every duty injoin'd will promt him to examine how he has perform'd ; every fin forbid, will call him to recollect how guilty he has bin ; every pathetick ftrain of devotion will kindle his zeal, or at leaft upbraid his coldnefs : every heroick example will excite his emulation. In a word, every part of Scripture will, if duly appli'd, contribute to fome good and excellent end. And when a thing is proper for fuch noble purpofes, can it be the part of a wife man to apply it only to mean and trivial ? Would any but an Idiot waft that Soveraign Liquor in the wafhing of his feet, which was given him to expel poifon from his heart ? And are not we guilty of the like folly when we apply Gods word to ferve only a ludicrous humor : and make our felves merry with that which was defign'd for the moft

F f ferious

serious and most important purpose; the salvation of our souls. And indeed who ever takes any lower aim than that, and the vertues preparatory to it in his study of Scripture, extremely debases it.

58. LET us therefore keep a steady eie upon that mark, and press towards it as the Apostle did, *Phil.* 3. 14. *walk by that rule* the holy Scripture proposes; faithfully and diligently observe its precepts, that we may finally partake its promises. To this end continually pray we, in the words of our holy mother the Church, unto Almighty God, who has caus'd all holy Scripture to be written for our learning; that we may in such wise hear them, read, mark, learn, and inwardly digest them, that by patience and comfort of his holy Word, we may embrace and ever hold fast the blessed hope of everlasting Life, which he has given us in our Savior Jesus Christ.

THE

THE CONTENTS.

SECTION.

FINIS.

Im TheStory

personalised classic books

"Beautiful gift.. lovely finish.
My Niece loves it, so precious!"

Helen R Brumfieldon

⭐⭐⭐⭐⭐

UNIQUE GIFT

FOR KIDS, PARTNERS
AND FRIENDS

Timeless books such as:

Kids

Alice in Wonderland • The Jungle Book • The Wonderful Wizard of Oz
Peter and Wendy • Robin Hood • The Prince and The Pauper
The Railway Children • Treasure Island • A Christmas Carol

Adults

Romeo and Juliet • Dracula

Highly Customizable   **Change** Books Title   **Replace** Characters Names with yours   **Upload** Photo that Inside page!   **Add** Inscriptions

Visit

Im TheStory .com

and order yours today!